How New Risk Management Helps Leaders Master Uncertainty

How New Risk Management Helps Leaders Master Uncertainty

Robert B. Pojasek, PhD

BEP BUSINESS EXPERT PRESS

How New Risk Management Helps Leaders Master Uncertainty

First published in 2019 by
Business Expert Press, LLC
222 East 46th Street, New York, NY 10017
www.businessexpertpress.com

ISBN-13: 978-1-94999-160-4 (paperback)
ISBN-13: 978-1-94999-161-1 (e-book)

Business Expert Press Business Law and Corporate Risk Management Collection

Collection ISSN: 2333-6722 (print)
Collection ISSN: 2333-6730 (electronic)

Cover and interior design by Exeter Premedia Services Private Ltd., Chennai, India

First edition: 2019

10 9 8 7 6 5 4 3 2 1

Printed in the United States of America.

Abstract

Risk is the effects of uncertainty on the ability of an organization to meet its strategic objectives. The effects of uncertainty are expressed as opportunities and threats. Most people associate risk with hazards and losses (i.e., pure risk). Unlike pure risk, uncertainty risk is not insurable because of its upside risk opportunities. These opportunities are identified by scanning the internal and external operating environments of an organization. Highly ranked opportunities can be developed to help offset the threats to the organization. Risk management is a key element of the open-sourced, "high-level structure" developed by the International Organization for Standardization. This structure for managing important organizational programs has been adopted by over 180 country standard-setting organizations.

The high-level structure accountability for risk management has been assigned to an organization's "top leader." This concise book provides the information needed by that leader to identify opportunities and threats and decide on the appropriate risk response in an uncertain world. The two most widely used risk management standards are presented to demonstrate that an organization can use either one or a combination of the two standards to help manage the effects of uncertainty on the organization. Some organizations use this information to create a risk management program that is unique to their organization. It is fool worthy to attempt to run an organization without formal uncertainty risk management. Let this guide help you find your way in this uncertain world.

Keywords

High-Level Structure; Risk; Risk Management; Opportunities and Threats; Organizational Objectives; COSO ERM:2017 Enterprise Risk Management Standard; ISO 31000:2018 Risk Management Standard; Top Leader's Accountability

Contents

Reviewers Notes

Wayne Muscarello

This book is exactly what I would expect to read if I were an executive. It clearly lays out the terms of risk management, provides a baseline understanding of the components of risk management and offers a reference to the tools that should be used.

The flow of the information in the book is written to guide you through the entire process in order. The material provides the reader with a background on risk management which adds a bit of interest to the subject matter.

The thing I liked best about the book is the concise information the user of presented in bullet points to easily allow the reader the ability to pull the information into a slide deck for a presentation. Plus, it allows the reader to quickly find the information.

The processes and information in the book are exactly what is used in most organizations today. It's current and relevant to how large and small organizations function. Experienced risk managers will know that the information captured in the book is indicative of how risk management is implemented at most organizations.

Most executives in the United States are more familiar with COSO than the ISO standards. The book gives them reinforcement on COSO and possibly the first glimpse of what ISO 31000:2018 is about. The CRO of a company would easily see how useful the information is and could effortlessly pull text from the chapter to create slides for a presentation.

I don't know of any company that has formal risk management competency requirements for any staff except IA (Internal Audit). The book reminds organizations to add some type of risk competency and awareness for employees as part of the onboarding process.

Lawrence Heim

The book offers a detailed analysis of integrating the ISO 31000:2018 risk management system and the COSO ERM: 2017 enterprise risk management system into company operations and management. Dr. Pojasek's comparison and contrast of ISO 31000 and the more familiar COSO framework gives helpful and practical tips for integration or establishing an enterprise risk management standard from the information derived from the two standards.

Ralph Jarvis

Dr. Robert Pojasek is a pragmatic thought leader in sustainability and integrates sustainably developed principles into corporate business practices. This book flows easily, directly and connects from the top level to the next levels. It conveys a logical step-by-step approach for implementing risk management within the high-level structure used today by the top corporations around the world. Each topic emphasized is interwoven and relates to themes previously discussed. It provides the reader a signal to revisit those chapters to refresh their understanding. Dr. Pojasek demonstrates an effective model identifying and illustrating the international risk management methods. But don't be surprised when he expands other related insights and underpinnings, as well!

Preface

Many people believe that "risk" only has negative consequences. While this is true with "pure risk," you will learn that "context risk" addresses the "effects of uncertainty" with potential adverse effects (threats) and potential beneficial effects (opportunities). Every organization experiences both kinds of risk. They manage pure risk with the help of insurance and the placement of "controls" on the operations. Context risk involves the searching of the external and internal environments of the organization for "opportunities and threats." Context risks are managed with standards, such as COSO ERM:2017 and/or ISO 31000:2018. These copyrighted standards are designed to help an organization's leader decide "what" they need to do in order to conform. However, more importantly, the standards often suggest "how" the organization can meet the standard.

In this book, we present the clauses in the standard that describe the "what." This information can be found on the Internet since both standards have published open source summaries of the standards. This concise book strongly recommends that the top leader purchase the standards (see the book list provided in Chapter 2) to determine how to best determine the options (the "how") for implementing the standards in their organization. The limited use of information from the standards has been cited in text with endnotes provided for each chapter. This should help the reader identify the complete citation that can be found in the references. "Fair Use" also allows this book to support risk management courses taught at the master's degree level.

The first chapter in this book should help the reader understand the many topics and perspectives involved in when someone is evaluating different kinds of risk in the organization. In the second chapter, the reader will learn about risk management. It only deals with context risk and the "effects of uncertainty." Pure risks are "controlled" to manage risk and contain the costs of insurance.

Chapters 3 to 5 examine how ISO 31000:2018 systematically addresses opportunities and threats in an organization. This standard has a well-defined implementation approach. Sections of COSO ERM:2017 are presented that work quite well in tandem with ISO 31000:2018. These standards are rarely integrated with each other. Information in these chapters will enable the reader to use a purchased copy of the standards for creating a risk management program that works best for the organization.

Chapter 6 examines the remaining sections of COSO ERM:2017 and how they can be used in addition to ISO 31000:2018. Your organization now has a choice. It can use either standard, integrate the two standards, or use both standards to construct a unique risk management method that will work best for your organization.

Chapter 7 examines how risk management can be used with the ISO "high-level structure" that is used in all the ISO management systems. This high-level structure is an open-source document available on the Internet. Besides allowing organizations to integrate standards to have all the information in one place, they also offer a means for integrating risk management into the work that everyone does every day within the organization where they work.

No matter what direction is chosen, the person designated as the "top leader" of the organization should purchase the two standards. As stated earlier, these standards are written to provide useful copyrighted information on *how* best to use the standards. This is a big step beyond understanding *what* can be done with these two risk management standards. The standards provide much more detail than is presented in this concise book. You can locate the organizations that sell these two standards on the Internet. In Chapter 2, I have suggested a reading list on risk management for the top leader of an organization. This list is helpful since the ISO high-level structure holds the "top leader" fully accountable for obtaining objectives set by the organization. The responsibility of leadership to be held accountable for the use of risk management is highlighted in the additional readings that will help the organization move beyond the defensive posturing around different kinds of risk and the different ways that risk is managed. It will take a compelling vision of the "top leader" to overcome the indecisiveness and lead the way to a risk-aware culture that will be needed to find the opportunities that will help the organization offset the threats. Success is determined when the organization meets it strategic objectives that are derived from its mission statement.

I would like to thank the peer reviewers that provided clarity and new ideas that needed to be explored in this effort. They include:

- Lawrence Heim—ELM Sustainability Partners
- Ralph Jarvis—Jarvis Business Solutions LLC
- Charles Wayne Muscarello—IT Internal Audit Consultant

I would like to thank Tammy Wyche (Institute of Internal Auditors) for alerting me to the most recent COSO ERM:2017 standard and how risk management is currently used in internal auditing. John Wood, Esq. is an Editor for Business Expert Press. With his review and guidance, I was able to work with the editorial staff of Business Expert Press to complete this book so that you could use it with confidence to lead a risk management effort in your organization. I will host a microsite on this book at http://bringchangenow.com I will also publish new uses for the information in the book and engage in conversations with the people that are using the book and the outcomes of this work. Hopefully you will join in on that conversation and learn about specialized training that we will make available on the topic of risk and risk management.

Robert B. Pojasek, PhD
Strategic Impact Partners
Boston, MA USA
https://BringChangeNow.com

CHAPTER 1

Understanding Risk

Introduction

The Oxford Dictionary defines "risk" as a situation involving exposure to danger. Asking people for their definition of risk provides us with a variety of responses. Some of these responses focus on a concern for uncertainty or danger, while others refer to the financial consequences of unwanted events. Every organization faces some degree of risk every day. However, we normally focus on catastrophic events and whether the organization is properly covered by insurance protecting us from the consequences of these events.

Other sources of risk include the following[1]:

- The possibility of an unfortunate occurrence
- Doubt concerning the outcome of a situation
- Unpredictability
- Possibility of loss
- Needing to improve the ability to be an effective leader

These conceptions of risk help us understand risk broadly as the uncertainty of future events and their outcome for our organization.

Leading companies create or adopt frameworks for understanding risk and supporting risk management. Typically, the approach to understanding risk is one that supports the business and its internal and external context, while ensuring that risk management is embedded across the entire organization. This action requires an explicit management dialogue with every element of the organization and its key stakeholders. Generally, corporations do not like risk or uncertainty. In these organizations, new initiatives are carefully reviewed to either eliminate risk or mitigate that risk to levels acceptable to the organization. This situation makes these companies more vulnerable to disruption as entrepreneurial companies have a greater tendency to put risk aside or accept a higher risk tolerance to make an impact on how organizations conduct their business.

As a result, it is important for organization leaders to understand risk and uncertainty. There are manageable ways to understand risk without having to get confused by all the risk-naming conventions. The organization should conduct a thorough search for risks as a first step in a risk management program. This list needs to be updated whenever changes in the company occur or when circumstances relevant to the organization changes (e.g., governmental changes, economic instability, social trends, etc.). It is not necessary to build a complicated risk classification system. The major risk management program standards do not encourage the classification of risk. A few important concepts necessary to understand risk are presented as follows.

Pure Risk and Speculative Risk

A pure risk features a chance of a loss and no chance of a gain. People often use the word "risk" to describe a financial "loss." Losses result from: fires, floods, snow, hurricanes, earthquakes, lightning, and volcanoes. Within the business, losses include more complex matters, such as sickness, fraud, environmental contamination, terrorism, electronic security breaches, and strikes.

A risk is the possibility of a loss. A peril is the cause of a loss. Perils expose people and property to the risk of damage, injury or loss against which the organization often purchases insurance to cover the cost of that loss. Please note that the terms peril and loss are often mistakenly used interchangeably.

Insurance companies cover financial losses from pure risks that meet conditions: due to chance; definitiveness and measurability; statistical predictability; lack of catastrophic exposure; random selection; and loss exposure.

PURE RISK involves a chance of a loss and no chance of a gain. Organizations generally use insurance to deal with pure risk. Operational controls are used to reduce the total cost of insurance.

Pure risk can involve a hazard. A hazard is something that increases the probability that a peril will occur (e.g., ice-covered road). Hazards are a condition or a situation that makes it more likely that a peril will occur. The situations include physical hazards, operational hazards, and business hazards. Common hazards include chemicals, repetitive motions, and physical conditions (e.g., vibrations; noise; slips, trips and falls; ergonomics); and biological effects.

Speculative risks are activities that produce a profit or a loss. These kinds of activities include new business ventures, reputation protection, modifications to operations, and alternative means of transportation. All speculative risks are undertaken as a result of a conscious choice. Speculative risk lacks many of the core elements of insurability.

Financial and Non-financial Risk

Larger corporations focus on the financial risk of their operations. Financial risk refers to an organization's ability to manage its debt and financial leverage. It also refers to non-debt financial losses, like lawsuits, property losses, crime/fraud and cyber risk. To address these financial risks, organizations create performance measures which include cash flow, credit, earnings, equity, foreign exchange, interest rates, liquidity and financial reporting.

However to have a vibrant risk management program in an organization, it is important to consider the non-financial risks associated with the operations. Non-financial risk are events or actions, other than financial transactions, that can negatively impact the operations or assets of a company. Typical non-financial risk (see Figure 1.1) includes misconduct, technology, ignoring key external stakeholders, customers and employees.

However, there are some drawbacks associated with non-financial performance measures. It is costly to have to monitor a large amount of financial and non-financial information. In some cases, the cost is greater than the benefits. Having many performance measures requires maintaining and studying information from multiple sources. There is often a competition between maintaining a good set of measures and finding the time needed to spend more time engaging with stakeholders and serving the customers.

There are established and certifiable means of measuring financial performance measures. However, this is not the case in non-financial

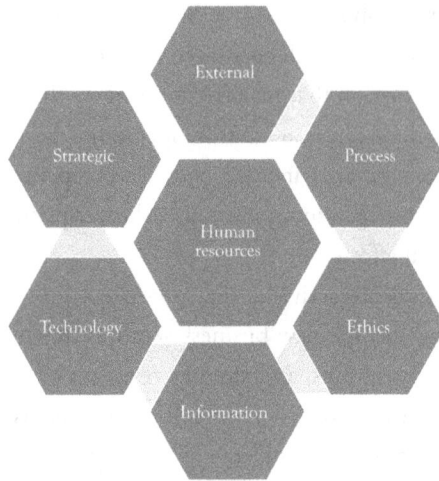

Figure 1.1 Non-financial risk[2]

measures. Evaluating performance or making tradeoffs between measure-
ments is difficult when some are measured in time, others are measured
in percentages or amounts, and a few are determined in arbitrary ways.
Furthermore, not all stakeholders understand, or hold a similar appreciation of, non-financial measures. Lastly, accounting systems are designed
around financial measures and do not handle non-financial concepts well.
(see Figure 1.2).

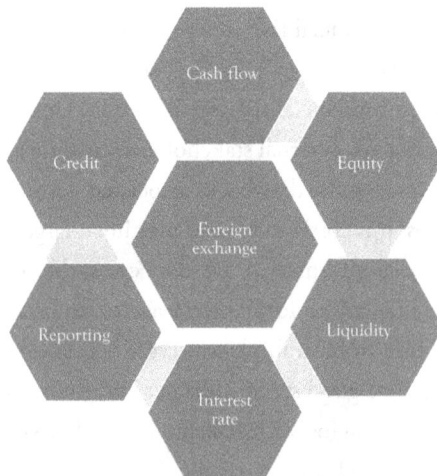

Figure 1.2 Financial risk[3]

Although non-financial measures are receiving more attention in risk management programs, organizations should not simply copy the measures from other organizations.[4] The choice of the non-financial measures should be unique to each company and linked to organizational strategy and meeting the organizations explicit objectives and other value drivers.

Opportunities and Threats

With the advent of the practice of risk management (i.e., different than hazards control) in the 1990s, there has been a shift to using opportunities and threats as a means of managing risks of an organization. As noted earlier, the traditional view of risk is negative. This view characterizes all risks as "threats" with adverse consequences on the ability of the organization to meet its objectives. However, there is a possibility that uncertainty in the internal and external operating environments can create an "opportunity" which has a beneficial effect on achieving organizational objectives. This is consistent with the more recent view of risk as being the "effects of uncertainty" on the ability of the organization to meet its business objectives. The nature of uncertainty and its effect on objectives can change over time. As a result, the risk will change. What is found in uncertainty today, may not be true in the future. Since most business strategic objectives are established for a five- to ten-year timeframe, it is very important to continuously monitor and measure the operating environment.

The International Organization for Standardization (ISO) defines "effect"[5] (as in the effects of uncertainty) as "a deviation from the expected—positive or negative." Opportunities that are brought to light are often not the opportunities that might have been already known to the organization. They are challenging opportunities, so the thought of them being a "risk" is very apropos. Most organizations that are using the opportunities and threats in their risk management program, select a couple of the highest ranked opportunities and seek to exploit them in lieu of simply treating the top threats that have been identified. It is important to remember that you should not use the word "risk" interchangeably with the word "threat."

Context Risk

The context risk is defined as follows[6]:

The effect of uncertainty on objectives. An effect is a deviation from the expected. It can be positive, negative, or both. An effect can arise as a result of a response, or failure to respond to an opportunity or to a threat related to objectives. Risk is usually expressed in terms of risk sources, potential events, their consequences and their likelihoods.

Establishing the context of an organization is concerned with the understanding of the external and internal operating environments to identify the risks (i.e., opportunities and threats) that would be of concern to the company. The information obtained from determining the context risk will help identify the structure for the risk management activities described in Chapter 2. Careful delineation of the context risk is needed to[7]:

- Clarify the organization's objectives.
- Identify the operating environments within which the objectives are pursued.
- Specify the scope and objectives for the risk management, boundary conditions and the outcomes.
- Identify the criteria that will be used to measure the risks.
- Define a set of key elements that will be used to structure the risk identification and assessment process.

The context is used to establish, implement, maintain and continually improve the organization's high-level structure.[8] Creating an understanding of the context risks provides an appreciation of all the factors that could exert an influence on the ability of an organization to meet its objectives (i.e., outcomes). The organization determines those opportunities and threats that need to be addressed and managed.

Context Risk is the effects of uncertainty on the ability of the organization to meet its objectives. These risks consist of both opportunities and threats.

Risk management—coordinated activities to direct and control an organization with regard to risk.

External Context and Stakeholders

The external environment is part of the organization's context. It is anything, including the external stakeholders, in the external operating environment that can influence the organization's ability to achieve its objectives.[9] The PESTLE tool (an acronym of influences that stands for political, economic, sociological, technological, legal and environmental) provides a risk classification system for the external context.[9] There are large numbers of possible "factors" associated with each "influence" defined by the PESTLE tool. External risk comprises both opportunities and threats that are not wholly within the control of the organization. In some cases, the organization would have to work with external stakeholders to realize these opportunities and threats.

The PESTLE tool is not mentioned by name in the ISO 31000:2018 risk management standard. However, it is mentioned in the COSO ERM:2017[11] and in the Australian standard that was used in the process of writing ISO 31000:2018.[12]

PESTLE analysis is a widely used tool for searching for opportunities and threats associated with an organization and its supply chain. It creates a conversation about opportunities and threats that can work well to engage external stakeholders as required by ISO 31000:2018 and COSO ERM:2017. It is important to use a practice known as "sense making" so that information gathered during screening is clearly understood by those responsible for conducting the scanning activity and to help the survey team record this information in the knowledge management system.[13]

Every opportunity and threat catalogued by the PESTLE search team has an external stakeholder associated with it.[14] ISO 31000:2018 requires stakeholders to be directly involved in the risk assessment process. This helps engage these stakeholders as a front-line effort to keep the scanning of the external environment up to date at all times and to help the organization understand the significance of the factors found in each of the influences. These stakeholders can also help assess the "materiality" of opportunities and threats for the sustainable development program.

Internal Context and Stakeholders

The internal context can be determined by scanning the situation within the organization with a TECOP tool[15] (an acronym of influences that stands for technical, environmental, commercial, operational and political). This tool is widely used in the project management field.[16] Like the PESTLE tool, this TECOP scanning tool is designed to help understand the influences and factors (i.e., subset of activities within each influence) affecting the operation of the organization and to be able to identify the opportunities and threats associated with the factors.

SWIFT Tool

Many people responsible for characterizing the internal and external context use a "structured what-if technique" (SWIFT)[17] to ask questions that help find the "factors" and the opportunities and threats. This tool also has wide use for those working with hazard risks. By understanding the process, it is possible to create internal controls to lower the "pure risk" and support the risk management effort. The SWIFT tool involves the use of process maps to make sure that all the main processes and their supporting processes are covered both in the SWIFT activity and in the TECOP activity.

Strategy Risk

All organizations find themselves dealing with a wide range of uncertainties every day. The opportunities and threats associated with uncertainty may impact the organization's ability to execute its strategies and achieve its strategic objectives.[18] These opportunities and threats can ultimately affect shareholders' and/or stakeholders' view the long-term viability of the organization.

The organization's strategy (whether derived explicitly or implicitly) is the process to establish and maintain the strategic objectives of the organization. Failure of the strategy effort to manage opportunities and threats while establishing and maintaining objectives is just as important in having them impact the strategic objectives after they are created.

Leaders need to first think about the strategy that their organization is using to achieve its objectives. They can then use that knowledge to manage opportunities and threats that could potentially be significant enough to threaten the strategy and improve the ability to meet the objectives.

Strategic risks are very broad in practice. Most risk managers do not focus on strategic opportunities and threats. The focus should be on the exposure of the strategy in its ability to create the most important opportunities for the organization.

Risk and Risk Management Vocabulary

When dealing with risk in the context of an organization, it is important to share a common language regarding risk and risk management. The ISO has created an "open source document" for this purpose.[19] Some of the ISO management system standards slightly modify these terms. Company communications concerning risk management efforts must use an agreed upon vocabulary. The top leader should make sure that these terms are consistently used both within the organization and when seeking engagement with the stakeholders.

Hazard risks undermine objectives and often have a high level of significance in some industries. These hazard risks are closely related to insurable risks. Remember that a hazard (or pure risk) can only have a negative outcome. The occupational health and safety management system, ISO 45001:2018, is very careful in maintaining information on both hazard risk and the risk associated with the effects of uncertainty. Consider the wording in this standard's Section 6.1.2.2.[20]

"The organization shall establish, implement and maintain a process(es) to:

(a) assess OH&S risks from the identified hazards, while taking into account the effectiveness of existing controls;
(b) determine and assess the other risks related to the establishment, implementation, operation and maintenance of the OH&S management system."

All management systems will need to separate the hazard risks in a similar manner.

Upside of Risk

There are many ways to look at what people refer to as "the upside of risk." It can represent the potential to eliminate a degree of uncertainty by exploiting an identified opportunity. When successful, the organization would be ahead of its plan to meet its strategic objectives. By adding opportunities to the risk management definition, you would think that organizations would be embracing this chance to be on the upside of risk. But another explanation would have the organization undertake activities that it would not otherwise have the "appetite" to undertake. No matter how you think of the upside of risk, everyone can agree that this is a place that you wish to be.

Investors believe that when an organization accepts a substantial risk, there is chance that there could be a greater opportunity. The ISO management system standards have some problem with the use of risk in this phrase since it is assuming that the risk is equal to threat. To get around this point, the standards have redefined "risk and opportunity" to mean[21]: "potential adverse effects (threats) and potential beneficial effects (opportunities)."

While there are a lot of nuances associated with opportunities and threats, organization's will be seeking the ability to use opportunities to offset threats.

Documenting Risk

It is important to document each of the activities described in this chapter. Organizations used to maintain detailed "risk registers" with information on the risks that have been identified. However, this terminology was associated with tables and spreadsheets that are no longer in widespread use. Now companies maintain a "risk profile," with the risk identification process. This document provides a composite view of the risk assumed at a level of the organization, or aspect of the business, that positions management to consider the types, severity, and interdependencies of risks. It also states how these risks may affect performance relative to the strategy and objectives.[22]

The major tools used today for gathering information on opportunities and threats are the PESTLE and TECOP analyses. The information from these scans and the use of the SWIFT tool must be documented and reviewed by the top managers to assess the effectiveness of the risk management program. The concept and practice of risk management is presented in the next chapter.

Notes

1. Insurance Institute of Ireland (2014).
2. Baker (2018).
3. Baker (2018).
4. Ittner and Larcker (2000).
5. ISO (2015a).
6. ISO (2015).
7. Standards Australia, Standards New Zealand (2004).
8. ISO (2015).
9. COSO (2017).
10. Hopkin (2012).
11. COSO (2017).
12. Standards Australia, Standards New Zealand (2004).
13. Pojasek (2017).
14. Pojasek (2017).
15. Pojasek (2017).
16. Hillman (2014).
17. ISO (2009).
18. Anderson and Frigo (2014).
19. ISO (2009a).
20. ISO (2018a).
21. ISO (2015a).
22. COSO (2017).

CHAPTER 2

Managing Risk

Introduction

Risk is inherent in every activity performed within an organization.[1] We manage risk continuously, whether this is done consciously or done without realizing it. Risk management (see Figure 2.1) is an iterative process consisting of well-defined steps that support better decision making within the organization. Here are the basics of risk management:[2]

- Organizations of all types and sizes face external and internal factors and influences that make it uncertain whether they will achieve their objectives.
- Managing risk assists organizations in setting strategy, achieving objectives, and making informed decisions.
- Managing risk is part of organizational governance and leadership and is fundamental to how the organization is managed at all levels. It contributes to the improvement of management systems.
- Managing risk is part of all activities associated with an organization and includes interaction with all stakeholders.

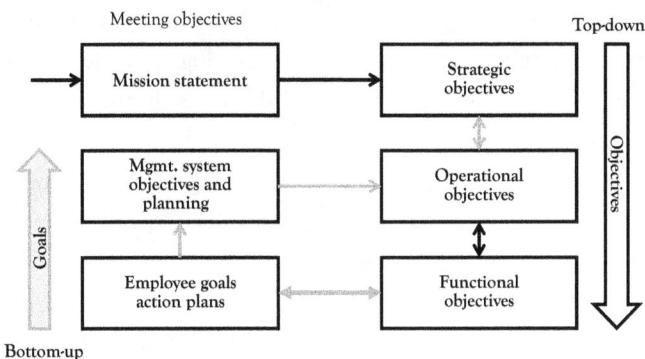

Figure 2.1 Meeting Strategic Objectives[3]

- Managing risk considers the external and internal context of the organization, including human behavior and cultural factors.

These components might already exist in full or in part within the organization; however, they might need to be adapted or improved so that managing risk is efficient, effective and consistent.

The risk management process can be applied to any situation where an undesired or unexpected outcome could be significant or where opportunities and threats have been identified. All decision-makers need to know about possible outcomes and take steps to control their impact on the organization. Here is what the top leaders must get right[4]:

- Managing risk involves opportunities and threats.
- Managing risk requires critical thinking.
- Managing risk requires the organization to be proactive rather than reactive.
- Managing risk requires accountability on the top manager's part.
- Managing risk requires engagement with the internal and external stakeholders.
- Managing risk requires a balance between the cost of avoiding threats or enhancing opportunities and the benefits to be gained.

Risk is an integral part of good business practice in an organization. A structured risk management process enables leaders to improve outcomes by identifying and analyzing the wide range of issues and providing a systematic way to make informed decisions. It also enhances and encourages the identification of opportunities to be used in part to offset some of the threats. The principles of managing risk remain generic in nature and largely independent of any individual type of organizational structure.

The purpose of risk management is the creation and protection of value.

Some of the benefits of risk management include[5]:

- Avoiding surprises by achieving a degree of resilience through preparedness and planning.
- Improving opportunity-seeking behavior.
- Improved planning, performance and effectiveness.
- Achieving benefits in economy and efficiency.
- Improved engagement of internal and external stakeholders.
- Improved information for decision making.
- Investors, lenders, insurers, suppliers, and customers are drawn to organizations that are known to have a sound process of managing risk.
- Improved accountability, assurance and governance, no matter what size the organization.

Brief History of Risk Management

While the recorded history of risk dates to the Code of Hammurabi (i.e., a Babylonian law code) around 1750 BC, risk management began to be studied at the end of World War II. It was during the 1950s that the cost of different types of insurance coverage became very expensive. During the 1960s, the field of corporate risk management began to grow. Contingency plans were developed my many companies within their business continuity plan and disaster recovery plans. There was also an emphasis on loss prevention and safety management as people moved away from risk financing for speculative risks. The first academic books on risk management were published in 1963[6] and 1964.[7]

During the 1970s, self-insurance and risk retention practices developed within organizations. Captive insurance companies came into existence. There were considerable developments in the risk management approach adopted by occupational health and safety practitioners. During this time the concept of "total cost of risk" became important. As this approach became established, it also became obvious that there were many risks facing organizations that were not insurable. Self-protection activities became very important. Accident prevention became the most natural form of self-protection. Precaution is a form of self-protection was applied to suspected, but undefined events, for which the probabilities and financial consequences are unknown. All protection and prevention activities are part of risk management.

Standards of Australia began the process of creating the first national risk management system standard in 1990. This led to the publication of AS/NZS 4360 in 1995. This standard was updated in 1999 and again in 2004. With this milestone, corporate governance and listing requirements from some of the stock exchanges encouraged directors to place greater emphasis on what they called, "enterprise risk management" (ERM). The first Chief Risk Officers (CROs) were appointed around this time. However, their focus was on financial risk rather than non-financial risks. Operational risk management started to grow in this period.

During the 2000s, financial services firms were encouraged to develop internal risk management systems and capital models. There had been a rapid growth of CRO positions in energy companies, banks, and insurance companies. Boards were investing more time in ERM due to the enactment of the "Sarbanes-Oxley Act of 2002" in the United States and similar legislation in a number of other countries. This wave of legislation required publicly traded companies to report risks to the government (e.g., US Securities and Exchange Commission Forms 10-K and 40-F). Financial institutions developed internal risk management models to protect themselves from unanticipated risks. At the same time, governance of risk management became essential and integrated risk management was introduced for non-financial risks.

However, all these regulations, rules, and risk management methods were not enough to prevent the financial crisis that began in 2007. It was not necessarily the regulation of risks and governance rules that were inefficient, but rather their application and enforcement. There is no doubt that the application of risks management tools and techniques failed to prevent the global financial crisis. This event was brought about by the failure to correctly apply risk management processes and procedures, rather than inherent defects in the risk management approach.

The Process of Risk Management

Risk management now consists of well-defined steps that, when taken in sequence, support better decision making by contributing a deeper insight into risks and their impacts to the organization. The risk management process can be applied to any situation where an undesired or unexpected outcome could be significant or where opportunities are identified. Decision makers need to use the standards to help them understand possible outcomes and take steps to control their impact—at the upside or the downside of risk.

With the uptake of the use of formal risk management systems, the practice is becoming an integral part of good management practice. To optimize its effectiveness, risk management must become part of the organization's culture. It should be integrated into the organization's philosophy, practices, and business plans rather than being viewed or practices as a separate program. Once an organization achieve this distinction, risk management becomes the business of everyone in the organization.

If for some reason, it is not possible to integrate risk management across an enterprise, it can still be successfully applied within individual departments, processes or projects. There are risk management programs available for the enterprise level (e.g., COSO ERM:2017[8]) and similar programs for the project level.[9]

Risk management is informed by standards. A standard is a published document that sets out specifications and procedures designed to ensure that a process is fit for its purpose and consistently performs in the way it was intended. Standards tell you *what* it is that the organization should seek to do—standards do not tell you *how* to do it. The ISO 31000:2018 risk management standard involves managing risk to achieve an appropriate balance between successful utilization of opportunities to offset threats without having to "treat" these threats. This is an essential element of good organizational governance. Besides the standards, organizations still need to address pure risk with what are referred to as "controls."

The terminology[10] used in the ISO 31000:2018 has been determined to be acceptable across as wide a range of risks and risk management disciplines by the ISO technical committee. This committee also made an effort to avoid words that have slightly different meanings in different kinds of risk management. These words have been replaced by words that might be less commonly used in current practice but could be defined to have a precisely common meaning. Some of the veteran risk managers, especially those that started working with pure risks, still object to some definitions. The effort to harmonize the descriptions is an ongoing effort whenever a new or revised standard is released. Even the COSO ERM:2017 made a big step toward using processes and descriptions that are harmonized with ISO 31000:2018.

Importance of Leadership in Risk Management

The "High-Level Structure" (Annex SL)[11] is being used by the International Organization for Standardization (ISO) to define the importance of leadership in all the management systems issued under its authority. Here's how top leaders demonstrate their leadership and commitment with respect to risk management in an organization:[12]

- Taking responsibility and accountability for the prevention of loss and hazards associated with the organization's priority pure risks.
- Ensuring that the risk management policy and related risk management objectives are established and are compatible with the strategic direction of the organization.
- Ensuring the integration of the risk management requirements into the organization's business processes across all functions, departments and operations.
- Ensuring that the resources needed to establish, implement, maintain and improve the risk management activities are available.
- Communicating the importance of effective risk management and of conforming to the risk management program requirements.
- Ensuring that risk management efforts achieve intended outcome(s).
- Directing and supporting employees to contribute to the effectiveness of the risk management program.
- Ensuring and promoting continual improvement of this program.
- Developing, leading, and promoting a culture in the organization (see Chapter 3) that supports intended outcomes of the risk management efforts.

- Working directly with internal and external stakeholders in all the risk management processes.
- Ensuring the organization establishes and implements a process for engagement and consultation of the internal and external stakeholders throughout the risk management process.

Risk management is typically focused on the context risks described in Chapter 1. However, it is important to maintain efforts to control the risks associated with the hazards and loss activities also identified in Chapter 1.

> Risk management should be a part of, and not separate from, the organizational purpose, governance, leadership and commitment, strategy, objectives and operations.

Controlling Risk

When dealing with "pure risk," most organizations apply risk management using "controls" within an internal auditing program and through engineering, physical, chemical, training and administrative controls. The Committee of Sponsoring Organizations of the Treadway Commission (COSO) published "Internal Control—Integrated Framework" in 1992. This document is widely used for designing and implementing internal control and assessing the effectiveness of internal control. The current version of this important document was published in 2013.[13] The original framework focused on the financial reporting category of objectives. The newer version also examines non-financial aspects of risk and internal reporting. Controls help the organization mitigate risks to acceptable levels.

The system of internal control within an organization is an important component in the process of controlling risk. Internal control methods, processes, and checks that are in place to ensure that elements of the organization's operations meet objectives. Internal controls can be the actions taken by management to plan, organize and direct the performance of enough actions to provide reasonable assurance that objectives will be achieved.[14] In ISO 31000, this is referred to as the "risk context."

When designing effective internal controls, the organization should look at arrangements in place to achieve the following[15]:

- Maintenance of reliable systems
- Timely preparation of reliable information
- Safeguarding of assets
- Optimum use of resources
- Communicating with employees about controls and providing them with training
- Preventing and detecting fraud and error

Effective financial controls are an important and well-established element of control. This helps ensure that the organization is not unnecessarily exposed to financial risks and that financial information used within the business and for public reporting is reliable.

An effective system of internal control demands more than rigorous adherence to policies and procedures. It requires the use of judgment. Management and boards of directors use judgment to determine how much control is enough. Management and staff use judgment every day to select, develop, and deploy controls across the organization. Auditors apply judgment as they monitor and assess the effectiveness of the system of internal controls.[16]

Control of Hazard Risks

There are pure risks that require internal controls to help maintain an acceptable cost of insurance. These risks include[17]:

- Financial risks—Fraud and historical liabilities
- Chemical management system risks
- Infrastructure risks—Occupational health and safety and property fire protection
- IT security
- HR risks
- Legal risks—Contract language, disclaimers and limits of liability clauses

- Control of brand protection and environmental integrity
- Third party risks with controls such as product labels
- Contract services risks
- Marketplace risks—Technology developments and regulatory risks

These examples provide an overview of the wide range of hazard risks that can affect an organization. The constant evaluation of controls will result in benefits for the organization. It will ensure that controls are effective in producing the result that is required and controlling the risk to the expected level set out in the risk management policy. In addition, the efficiency of the existing controls can be evaluated, so the company can decide whether the current level of control is adequate and cost-effective.

Creating the Leader's Risk Management Library

There are several important external documents that the top leader must be familiar with to guide their role in directing the risk management activities of the organization. These documents consist of the following:

- ISO 31000:2018 Risk Management Standard[18]
- AS/NZS HB 436:2013 Companion to AS/NZS ISO 31000:2009[19]
- COSO ERM:2017 Enterprise Risk Management Standard[20]
- ISO Guide 73:2009 for Risk Management Terms[21]
- Pojasek, R.B. (2017). "Organizational Risk Management and Sustainability: A Practical Step-by-Step Guide[22]"
- Hopkin, Paul (2012) "Fundamentals of Risk Management.[23]"

The top leader and the board of directors should be provided with training to hone their skills using the contents from the books listed previously to guide them in providing accountability to the organization as discussed in this book. Should the organization not have a board, the top leader(s) needs to be identified so that the accountability can be created. For multifacility organizations, it is prudent to have each facility general manager trained to establish accountability at that level in the organization. Each facility has a different context and the operations may lead to differences in the pure risks.

Transition to Core Values and Principles

We will now turn our attention to the use of the risk management standards dealing with the effects of uncertainty (Figure 2.2). Because this book focuses on non-financial impacts of risk, we will focus on the ISO 31000:2018 risk management standard. In many cases the COSO ERM:2017 supports or varies slightly from the ISO standard. Many organizations rely on standards to help build the credibility of their risk management program for their dealings with customers, their supply chain, and the engagement of all stakeholders.

Chapter 3 examines the "principles" of ISO 31000:2018 and how they contribute to the culture of the organization. COSO ERM:2017 has an alternative approach to risk that complements the ISO standard to

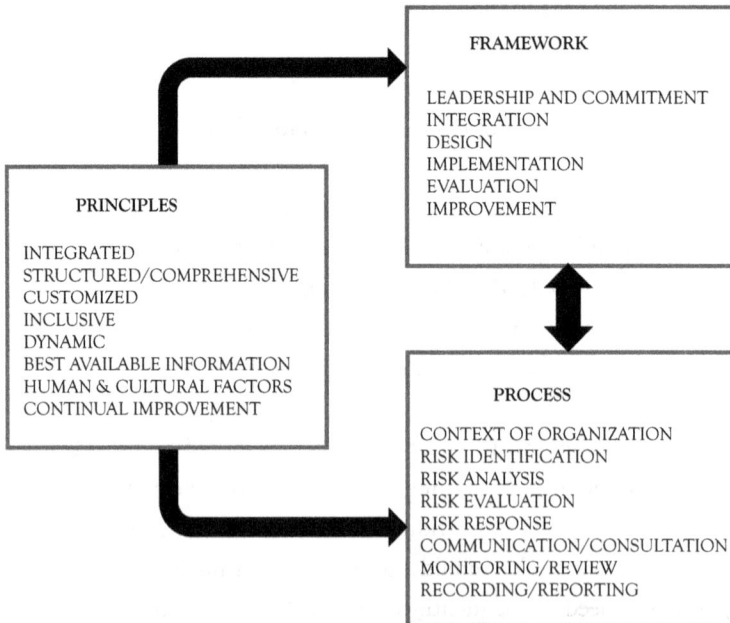

PRINCIPLES

INTEGRATED
STRUCTURED/COMPREHENSIVE
CUSTOMIZED
INCLUSIVE
DYNAMIC
BEST AVAILABLE INFORMATION
HUMAN & CULTURAL FACTORS
CONTINUAL IMPROVEMENT

FRAMEWORK

LEADERSHIP AND COMMITMENT
INTEGRATION
DESIGN
IMPLEMENTATION
EVALUATION
IMPROVEMENT

PROCESS

CONTEXT OF ORGANIZATION
RISK IDENTIFICATION
RISK ANALYSIS
RISK EVALUATION
RISK RESPONSE
COMMUNICATION/CONSULTATION
MONITORING/REVIEW
RECORDING/REPORTING

Figure 2.2 ISO 31000 Components[24]

provide a useful program for an organization addressing this element of risk management.

Chapter 4 examines the use of a risk management "framework."

Chapter 5 examines the use of the risk management process that is found both in ISO 31000 and COSO ERM:2018.

Notes

1. Standards Australia, Standards New Zealand (2013).
2. Pojasek (2017).
3. Pojasek (2017).
4. Pojasek (2017).
5. Pojasek (2017).
6. Mehr and Hedges (1963).
7. Williams and Hems (1964).
8. COSO (2017a).
9. Hillman (2014).
10. ISO (2014).
11. ISO (2009a).
12. ISO (2018a, 2017).
13. COSO (2013).
14. Hopkin (2012).
15. Hopkin (2012).
16. COSO (2013).
17. COSO (2013).
18. ISO (2018).
19. Standards Australia, Standards New Zealand (2013).
20. COSO (2017).
21. ISO (2014).
22. ISO (2018).
23. Pojasek (2018).
24. ISO (2018).

CHAPTER 3

Risk-Aware Culture

Introduction

COSO defines "enterprise risk management" as[1]:

> The culture, capabilities, and practices, integrated with strategy-setting and performance that organizations rely on to manage risks in creating, preserving and realizing value.

An organization is a social entity. People are important to organizations. Organizational theory provides a macro examination of people in the organizations because it analyzes the organizations as a unit. The point of studying organizations is to enable us to find ways to improve performance and effectiveness.[2] Improving an organization's effectiveness is not a simple matter. The diversity of people within an organization is often matched by the needs of these people to want different outcomes for that organization.[3]

Culture is developed and shaped by the people in the organization and manifested by what they say and do. The people interpret the organization's mission, strategy, and strategic objectives while putting risk management practices in place. Each person in an organization has a unique point of reference, which influences how they identify, assess, and respond to risk.[4] Risk management helps people make consistent decisions while understanding that culture plays an important role in shaping those decisions.[5]

A positive risk culture is one where people manage risk as an intrinsic part of their day-to-day work. Such a risk culture supports an open discussion about losses, hazards, opportunities and threats by encouraging people to express concerns and maintain processes to elevate concerns to the appropriate people within the organization.[6]

How Culture Is Influenced and Developed

An organization's culture is usually complex and influenced by several factors. It is generally recommended that before attempting to change an organization's culture, it is useful to first understand the ways in which the people in the organization are influenced. When establishing a formal risk management program for the first time, people can be influenced the most. During the introduction and induction procedures, people associated with risk management can clearly articulate the kind of behavior that is expected of people in the organization. It is also important to consider who conveys these messages and how they are delivered. The four key channels through which people are influenced and pick up cultural messages are[7]:

Role Models. The risk management behaviors that role models in the organization display will be influential on others. Role models instill values that become core beliefs about acceptable behavior in the organization.

Explicit Messages. Explicit messages that are incorporated in organizational policies and procedures create expectations and influence behavior. Throughout a person's career in an organization, they are provided with many instructions and guidelines. These guidelines explain how leaders view and manage risk.

Incentives. The way leaders are rewarded and recognized for displaying good risk management behaviors indicate how risk management is valued within the organization. Leaders will be unlikely to take appropriate risks if there is no incentive to do so or where risk taking is punished.

Symbols and Actions. The daily actions of senior leaders are noticed by the staff and are often mirrored by them. Small positive actions by these leaders to manage risk can take on much wider symbolic importance and can spread values across the organization.

Understanding the Current Risk Culture Status

The first step in developing a positive risk culture is understanding the organization's current risk culture (if already present) and how well it supports the organization's approach to managing risk. This can be achieved by breaking down risk culture into a few measurable attributes.

These measures provide a baseline against which attempts to shape the risk culture of an organization can be measured.[8]

One way to measure the current status of each of the indicators is to conduct a survey. This helps provide information on the current risk culture, but also provides a benchmark which can be used to measure progress over time.[9]

As an added benefit, survey results can also provide a detailed understanding of how the people think and act in relation to risk management. This is quite useful for identifying the root causes of undesirable attitudes and behaviors. It can also help find opportunities to improve the overall risk management process.

Another method to consider involves supplementing the questionnaires with interviews of the leaders in the organization. This helps to validate the results of the survey and uncovering any additional issues. Risk managers have found that interviewing can be particularly helpful in determining the current and desired risk culture.[10]

Determining the Future State of the Organization's Risk Culture

Once the reorganization's culture is understood, it is important to determine the future state of its risk culture. Using a risk maturity model provides a way to target areas that still need to be improved and to further determine what lies ahead. A self-evaluation program tracks the progress to a future state. The levels of maturity can be adjusted to further determine the next future state.

As with any other self-improvement program, it is important to determine what changes are the most critical and target them with practical and focused actions.[11] One common strategy is to review those areas where the risk management culture is particularly positive, to understand how this finding can be leveraged, and to identify what level of risk management maturity is most appropriate for the organization.

COSO Approach to Developing the Culture

Like the approach described earlier, COSO ERM: 2017 enables the organization to define the desired behaviors that characterize the organization's desire culture.[12] The COSO standard focuses on using the organization's core values. It is up to the members of the governance to define the desired culture of the organization and individuals who are directly associated with the organization. Core values drive the expected behaviors in day-to-day decision making to meet the stakeholders' interests. Establishing a culture embraced by all individuals associated with the organization, where people do the right thing at the right time, is critical to the organization to be able to seize opportunities and offset the threats in order to achieve the strategy and the strategic objectives.[13] Defining the culture does not imply a template approach to risk management. Nothing can stop the managers of some units from accepting more risk, while other managers are risk adverse.

Applying Judgment

Judgment is a function of an individual's personal experiences, risk appetite, capabilities and the level of information available. Management judgment is susceptible to bias whenever their own abilities to lead/manage a specific issue or avoid a potential risk. Behaviors within the organization may also lead to organizational bias that affects judgment. Group dynamics in meetings, communication styles of management, and recognition and acknowledgement affect individual's use of good judgment.

The use of judgment impacts the ability of an organization to navigate periods of disruption and resume normal operations more efficiently. Actions taken by the leaders to steer the organization out of a crisis depend on the accountability, behaviors, and decisions of individuals. Judgment also affects the extent to which innovation and the identification of opportunities are fostered within the organization. An organization that is characterized by prescriptive approaches and limited delegations of authority, may stifle innovation. An organization that places a stronger emphasis on risk-aware culture may rely more on management's judgment when making decisions that enhance values and in seeking new opportunities in line with the risk appetite of the entity.[14]

Aligning Core Values, Decision Making and Behaviors

The ability of an organization to successfully achieve its strategy and objectives is impeded when behaviors and decisions of individuals within the organization do not align with the core values. Such misalignment can result in a loss of confidence from stakeholders, inconsistent approaches, and lower than expected level of performance.

In a risk-aware culture, personnel know what the organization stands for and the boundaries within which they can operate. Within such an organization, the individuals can openly discuss and debate which opportunities (risks) should be taken to achieve the organization's strategy and objectives. The result being employee and management behaviors that are more consistently aligned with the organization's risk appetite.[15]

COSO Demonstrates Commitment to Core Values

Reflecting Core Values Throughout the Organization

Understanding the organization's core values is fundamental to risk management. Core values are reflected in actions and decisions applied throughout the organization. Without an understanding and a commitment to the core values, risk awareness can be undermined.[16]

Governance and leadership functions establish a common understanding of the core values. Paying attention to this responsibility sends a consistent message to the entire organization and entities with which it does business. Aligning the culture and the consistent messaging gives confidence to stakeholders that the organization is adhering to its core values and the pursuit of its strategic objectives.

Embracing a Risk Aware Culture

A company's leadership defines the characteristics needed to achieve the desired culture over time. The organization can develop a risk-aware culture by[17]:

- Maintaining strong leadership.
- Enforcing accountability for all actions.
- Aligning risk-aware behaviors and decision making with performance.
- Embedding risk management in decision making.
- Having open and honest discussions about risks facing the organization.
- Encouraging risk awareness across the entity.

Responding to Deviations in the Core Values

Establishing a culture in which management and personnel act according to desired behaviors is fundamental to risk management. Despite this, operational failures, scandals, and crises do occur. These damage reputations and threaten an organization's ability to achieve its strategic objectives.

The organization needs to send a clear message of what is acceptable and unacceptable behavior consistent with its core values. Deviations from standards of conduct must be addressed in a timely and consistent manner. The response to a deviation will depend on its magnitude as determined by leadership. This response may range from an employee being issued a warning to being put on probation to even being terminated. In all cases, expectations of risk-aware behavior, judgment, and decision making must remain consistent. Consistency ensures that the organization's culture is not undermined.[18]

ISO 31000 Approach to Developing the Culture

ISO 31000:2018 presents eight (8) principles to support the achievement of objectives through creation and protection of value. These principles provide guidance on the characteristics of efficient and effective risk management.[19] They also communicate how the organization improves performance while encouraging innovation. As such, the principles are the foundation for managing risk using the risk management framework and processes (see Figure 3.1).

These risk management principles are expressed as follows[20]:

1. Risk management is an integral part of all organizational activities.
2. A structured and comprehensive approach to risk management contributes to consistent and comparable results.
3. The risk management framework and processes are customized and proportionate to the organization's external and internal context, as well as being related to its objectives.
4. Appropriate and timely involvement of stakeholders enables their knowledge, views and perceptions to be considered. This results in improved awareness and informed risk management.

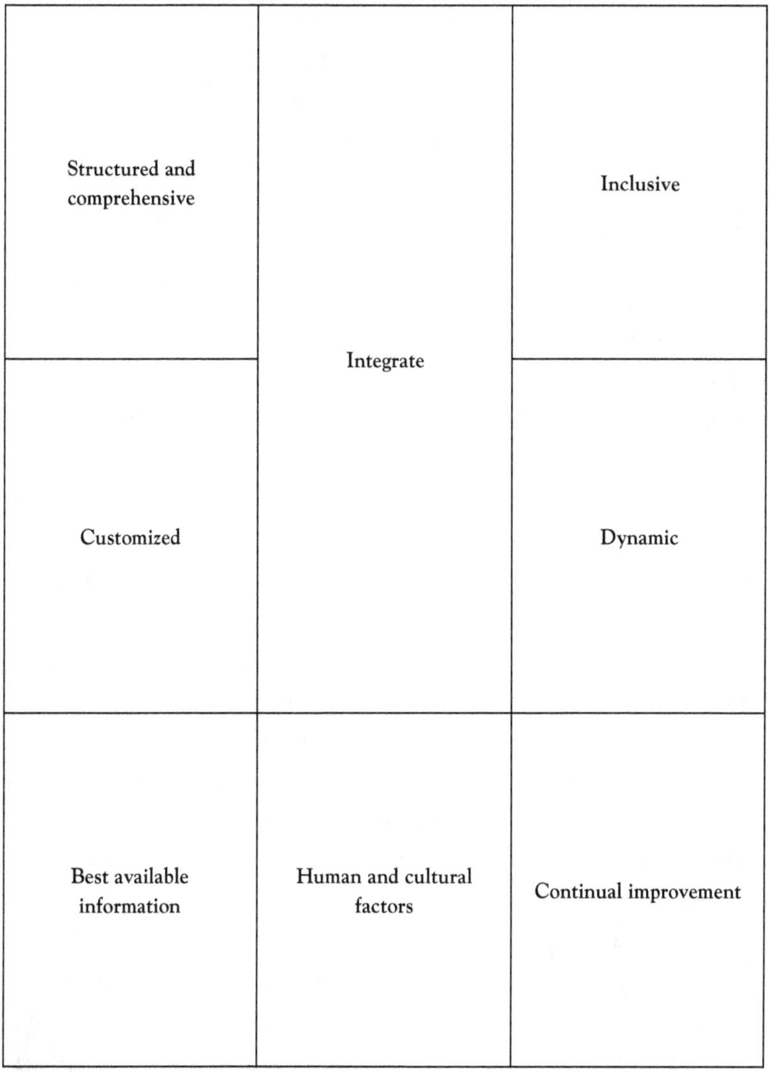

Structured and comprehensive		Inclusive
	Integrate	
Customized		Dynamic
Best available information	Human and cultural factors	Continual improvement

Figure 3.1 ISO 31000 Principles[21]

5. Risks can emerge, change, or disappear as an organization's external and internal context changes. Risk management anticipates, detects, acknowledges and responds to those changes and events in an appropriate and timely manner.

6. The inputs to risk management are based on historical and current information, as well as on future expectations. Risk management

explicitly takes into account any limitations and uncertainties associated with such information and expectations. Information should be timely, clear, and available to relevant stakeholders.

7. Human behavior and culture significantly influence all aspects of risk management at each level and stage.

8. Risk management is continually improved through learning and experience.

Unlike the components of the risk management framework (see Chapter 4) and the steps of the risk management process (see Chapter 5), the principles are not specified actions that must be taken, but rather essential underlying concepts and drivers. The principles thereby provide guidance to both the way the framework is structured, and how the risk management process is applied. They serve as indicators or characteristics that can be used diagnostically to evaluate the effectiveness of the risk management activities. Although the principles are expressed succinctly, the implications of each needs to be thoroughly understood in order to *give effect to them* on a continuing basis.[22]

Giving effect to the principles helps support the culture of risk management. Individuals need to become thoroughly conversant with each principle shown previously with the help of their supervisors. The "meaning" of a principle needs to become part of the employee's understanding of that principle in the context of their workplace. The individual then considers to what respects the principle would be likely to have application.[23]

For each principle, the individual reviews the present situation and considers which aspects of the organization's activities and processes generally, and risk management practices specifically, the principle applies. The individual then considers to what extent the principle is already evident and in which ways it could be given greater effect in the day-to-day work. It is advisable to use a simple methodology that allows a structured approach to consider in turn, for each principle, the organization's strategy, structure, methods and culture.[24] This does not need to be a comprehensive review. It is enough to use a systematic sampling approach that considers various levels and types of activities in the organization that are familiar to the individual. The leaders and governance need to look at more formal systems for their work.

The results are used for all of the principles to help improve the Framework and the way that the risk management process is applied. The organization should incorporate these changes into the annual risk management plan.

Ethical Trading

Ethical trading involves the actions taken by a company to require the suppliers to conform to a "supplier code of conduct." As companies face litigation on lapses in ethical trading, this effort has created an extension of the code of conduct detailed in this section. The targets of a typical ethical trading program[25] can be found in Box 3.1.

Box 3.1 Ethical trading

> 1. *Employment is freely chosen*
> 2. *Freedom of association*
> 3. *Working conditions are safe and hygienic*
> 4. *Child labor shall not be used*
> 5. *Living wages are paid*
> 6. *Working hours are not excessive*
> 7. *No discrimination is practiced*
> 8. *Regular employment is provided*
> 9. *No harsh or inhumane treatment is allowed*

Investors and other external stakeholders also demand that the supplier code of conduct include environmental quality, health and safety provisions, and business ethics safeguards to avoid fraud or illegal financial transactions (e.g., bribes or kickback payments). Risk management principles and risk-aware culture are necessary tools for those that seek to create management systems to prepare to comply with the ethical trading initiative.

It is important that ethical trading initiatives be combined with activities mentioned in this chapter. All the efforts described pay attention to the people in the organization. The concept is that by taking care of the people, you can improve the business. As was stated at the start of the chapter, organizations are social entities. People are at the foundation of all of the efforts that have been presented.

Risk Management Framework

The next section will explore the risk management "framework." This is the second of the three components of risk management that are included in ISO 31000:2018.

Notes

1. COSO (2017).
2. Pojasek (2017).
3. Pojasek (2017).
4. COSO (2017).
5. COSO (2017).
6. Australian Government, Dept of Finance (2016).
7. Australian Government, Dept of Finance (2016).
8. Australian Government, Dept of Finance (2016).
9. Australian Government, Dept of Finance (2016).
10. Australian Government, Dept of Finance (2016).
11. Australian Government, Dept of Finance (2016).
12. COSO (2017).
13. COSO (2017).
14. COSO (2017).
15. COSO (2017).
16. COSO (2017).
17. COSO (2017).
18. COSO (2017).
19. ISO (2018).
20. ISO (2018).
21. ISO (2018).
22. Standards Australia, Standards New Zealand (2013).
23. Standards Australia, Standards New Zealand (2013).
24. Standards Australia, Standards New Zealand (2013).
25. Ethical Trading Initiative (2018).

CHAPTER 4

Risk Management Framework

Introduction

The principles of risk management (see Chapter 3) and the framework are closely related. Each element of the risk management program deals with the concept of integration—the principles state that risk management should be integrated, while the framework insures that the integration takes place. The principles outline what must be achieved, and the framework provides information on how to achieve the required integration.[1]

An organization's ability to manage risk effectively depends on its intentions as well as its capability to achieve those intentions. A risk management framework sets the foundations and organizational arrangements for designing, implementing, monitoring, reviewing and continually improving the organization's risk management capability. This framework is part of the organization's system of governance and requires the diligent attention of top leadership of the organization.[2]

The content of this risk management framework is important because ineffective risk management can be linked to many organizational shortcomings[3]:

- Unclear or contradictory expectations from top leaders
- Lack of risk management capability
- Poor relationships with stakeholders
- Failure to include the necessary risk management practices in day-to-day activities and accountabilities of the top management
- No commitment to continually learn and improve

Effective risk management needs to provide clear intent and matching capability.

The governance of the organization is both accountable for and a key user of the risk management framework. Top leaders should use risk management to ensure that they, as well as the organization members, seize on appropriate opportunities and protect the organization against threats. Risk management also supports the governance's objectives that it has a fiduciary, reputational or a values-based responsibility to manage. Governance does this by making the framework align with the organization's mission and mandate and by being diligent and systematic in using the risk management process in its deliberations and decision making.[4] To be effective, the risk management framework must be fully integrated into the organization's everyday mode of operation.

If the organization's existing management practices and processes include components of risk management or if the organization has already adopted a formal risk management process as presented in Chapter 2, then these should be critically reviewed and assessed against the ISO 31000:2018 international standard. This review should determine their adequacy and effectiveness.[5]

Risk Management Framework

The risk management framework (see Figure 4.1) is not intended to prescribe an independent "management system." Instead, it seeks to assist the organization to integrate risk management into its overall system of management. The framework is what exists at any point in time, whether it is effective of ineffective.[6] It is not a single document, nor is it just a procedure, a copy of risk management software, AI or machine learning, a risk rating method or a database. All these items may form part of the framework.

This section of the book provides advice that will enable organization leaders to evaluate their existing risk management frameworks and, where necessary, to plan and implement improvements to enhance their risk management outcomes.[7]

Organizations and their people respond to a range of internal signals and other stimuli. Some of these, such as formal policies and plans, are explicit, while others, such as the organization's culture and brand, are implicit. Both can be equally powerful in influencing and directing the way that people in the organization behave and perform. However, they can undermine each other if they are not fully aligned.

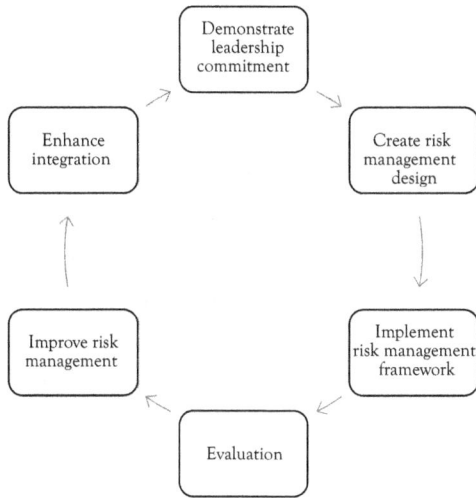

Figure 4.1 ISO 31000:2018 Risk management framework[8]

Establishing the intent is a matter of not just having a written mandate, but also providing explicit and implicit demonstration of commitment in a sustainable manner. Leaders should make it clear what is entailed and how it can be achieved.

Leadership and Commitment

The driving force in the risk management framework comes from top leaders (and the board of directors, where applicable) and should ensure that risk management is integrated into all organizational activities. This action should demonstrate leadership and commitment by[9]:

- Aligning risk management with the strategy, objectives and culture of the organization.
- Creating a risk management policy.
- Ensuring the necessary resources are allocated to this effort.
- Assigning authority, responsibility and accountability at appropriate levels within the organization.
- Recognizing and addressing all obligations of the organization.
- Addressing the risk appetite.
- Communicating the value of risk management to the organization and its stakeholders.

- Promoting the systematic monitoring of risks.
- Ensuring that the risk management framework remains appropriate.[10]

Risk management is manifested in every part of the organization's structure. When there are separate facilities, this will be reflected by different external context and the fact that the main office will be present in the internal context. Everyone in the organization has responsibility for managing risk.

Governance guides the course of the organization and the rules, practices, and processes to achieve its purpose. With this guidance, top management translates governance direction into the strategy and associated objectives required to achieve the desired levels of sustainable performance and long-term viability. Governance also determines the accountability and oversight roles. Integrating risk management into an organization is a dynamic and iterative process. It should be customized to meet the organization's needs and culture.

If the organization's intentions for the management of risk are not clearly communicated, these intentions are not likely to be achieved. Consistency in the approach of communication that is aligned with other essential programs is often more believable and has the effect of generating sustained engagement with the organization's intentions for risk management. Whatever the method, it must be clearly understood throughout the organization and believed and evident in the behavior of all.

Design of the Framework

When designing the framework for managing risk, the organization should examine and understand its external and internal context, as found in all ISO management systems. A great deal of emphasis is placed in the design activity on understanding the organization and its context (see Chapter 1).

Top leaders should articulate and demonstrate their continual commitment to risk management. This is generally accomplished through the creation of a risk management policy. It is designed to clearly convey an organization's objectives and commitment to risk management. The risk management policy should be communicated within the organization and to identified external stakeholders.

Top leaders should ensure that accountabilities, responsibilities and authorities for relevant roles with respect to risk management are assigned and communicated at all levels of the organization.

Improvements to the risk management framework need to be tailored to fit the organization to ensure that the resulting approaches are accepted, regarded as relevant, able to be integrated efficiently with minimum disruption, and will be responsive to ongoing change within the organization and its context.

The general characteristics of the organization to be considered in the design of the framework include[11]:

- Structure
- Governance practices and requirements
- Policies, internal standards and models
- Contractual requirements
- Strategic and operational systems
- Capability and resources
- Knowledge, skills, and intellectual property
- Information systems and flows
- Other organizational priorities and imperatives that can be perceived to compete with the organization's intentions for managing risk

These characteristics should be carefully tracked and checked on a periodic basis.

Accountability

As with every other aspect of organizational management, managing risk effectively requires people to have specific accountabilities, authorities and delegations, in addition to appropriate competence depending on their role in the organization.

There are two kinds of accountability for risk management[12]:

1. Accountabilities of those who are responsible for tasks associated with establishing, enhancing, or maintaining the risk management framework
2. Accountabilities of those who are responsible for the application of the risk management process or elements to support decision making in the strategic and day-to-day activities of the organization.

These accountabilities must be clearly expressed in terms of what is required, how performance will be measured, and how this will count in the overall assessment of the employee's performance. In the recruitment efforts, candidates should be required to demonstrate their proficiency in fulfilling the accountabilities of the role.

Accountabilities without matching skills are unlikely to produce the required performance. It is advisable to sponsor formal competency-based training for leaders and other employees with some level of awareness, risk management accountability and responsibility. By bringing the competency-based training to the business location, other people can take part to start building capability in these important areas.

Integration

All organizations manage risk. The methods and behaviors used may be effective or ineffective, efficient or inefficient, formal or informal, explicit or implicit. However, they will always be integrated in the strategic and day-to-day activities of the organization and be reflective of the organization's culture which may, unfortunately, conflict with the organization's objectives.

Many organizations are continually seeking to improve their risk management practices through the design of their framework but failing to appreciate that the only risk management approaches that will have a lasting effect are those that are an integral part of the organization's system of management. These improvements must also be supported and reinforced by the accountabilities presented earlier.

Integrated or embedded practices cannot be changed simply by issuing policies, procedures or requirements. They must be deliberately and thoughtfully integrated into the system of management by replacing or enhancing those that are already there. Plans for integrating changes to the framework must be explicit and should contain actions, timelines, and accountabilities. An integration effort must secure the necessary resources and consider competing priorities and any risks created by the effort.

As well as integrating the risk management framework into the organization's system of management, it will enhance effectiveness and efficiency if the framework also integrates approaches for managing all forms of risk (see Chapter 1). This can be challenging for some organizations that are accustomed to managing risk of different types in separate silos.[13] However, it is highly worth the effort.

Implementation

Once improvements to the risk management framework have been designed, it is necessary to plan and execute their implementation so that the risk management process can be applied to decision making throughout the organizational structure.

Organizations that are just beginning with the formal use of risk management need to establish how to integrate these components into its systems of management. This includes its approach to fundamental concepts that are likely to be improved though the diligent application of risk management methods. These organizational components of an organization include the following[14]:

- Strategic planning
- Budgeting
- Occupational health, safety and environment
- Recruitment and remuneration
- Delegation of authority
- Procurement and ethical sourcing
- Project management
- Capital raising and expenditure
- Marketing
- Stakeholder engagement
- Legal compliance
- Assurance
- Management reporting

For existing organizations, functions such as those shown earlier will need to be examined to identify where changes or enhancements will be required to ensure that the new framework for the management of risks has been integrated. Because risk is a result of decision making and acting on decisions, the design of the framework needs to take into account where, in the organization's activities, decisions are actually made and acted on. This is where risks need to be assessed and responded to.

Implementing a new or revised risk management framework in a new or existing organization requires careful planning.

Evaluation

In order to evaluate the effectiveness of the risk management framework, the organization needs to[15]:

- Periodically measure risk management framework performance against its purpose, implementation plan, risk results, and expected behavior.
- Determine whether it remains suitable to support the objectives of the organization.

The importance of an organization's operating system in meeting strategic objectives makes it clear that it is critical to have effective processes. The overall intention is to ensure that processes are effective, and the operations are always efficient. Effective processes also provide the means by which operations are changed and strategy is realized.[16]

Improvement

Organizations need to meet their strategic objectives in an uncertain world. Improvement is essential for an organization to maintain its operational performance and react to changes in the organization's internal and external context. It is critically important for the organization to continually monitor and adapt the risk management framework to address external and internal context changes. In this manner, the organization can enhance its value over the long term.[17]

The organization should continually improve the suitability, adequacy and effectiveness of the risk management framework and the way the risk management process is integrated into all its activities to address these. As improvement opportunities are identified, the organization should develop plans and tasks. These should be assigned to those accountable for implementing the risk management program. Once implemented, these improvements should contribute to the enhancement of risk management.

However, even with the framework operating as intended, if it can be improved, performance against objectives will be enhanced. Gaining greater competence in assessing and responding to risk or improving the way that risk information is made available to decision makers can make the organization more agile, and thus make it more resilient in the face of unexpected change.[18]

Working with the Risk Management Process

The risk management framework will ensure that the risk management process described in Chapter 5, is routinely applied to decision making so that the risk associated with decisions is effectively assessed, treated as necessary and that controls are routinely monitored and reviewed. An improved framework will help ensure that parts of the risk management process that have been conducted poorly in the past are improved.

Notes

1. IRM (2018).
2. Standards Australia and Standards New Zealand (2013).
3. Standards Australia and Standards New Zealand (2013).
4. Canadian Standards Association (2010).
5. Standards Australia and Standards New Zealand (2013).
6. Standards Australia and Standards New Zealand (2013).
7. Standards Australia and Standards New Zealand (2013).
8. ISO (2018).
9. ISO (2018).
10. ISO (2018).
11. Standards Australia and Standards New Zealand (2013).
12. Standards Australia and Standards New Zealand (2013).

13. Serrat (2010).
14. Standards Australia and Standards New Zealand (2013).
15. ISO (2018).
16. Pojasek (2017).
17. Pojasek (2018).
18. Standards Australia and Standards New Zealand (2013).

CHAPTER 5

Risk Management Process

Introduction

ISO 31000:2018 presents a risk management "process" that is featured in this chapter. The risk management process is explained in ISO 31000:2018 as being an integral part of management and decision making. This international risk management standard should be integrated into the structure, operations and processes of risk-aware organizations. It offers an iterative means of evaluating the effectiveness of the risk management efforts.

COSO ERM:2017 presents similar material under the heading of "Performance." The COSO ERM principles relating to performance include the following "principles":

- Identifies Risk—Principle 10
- Assesses Severity of Risk—Principle 11
- Prioritizes Risks—Principle 12
- Implements Risk Responses—Principle 13
- Develops Portfolio View—Principle 14

These processes are designed to be an integral part of the way organizations provide leadership and make decisions regarding how risk management is practiced at the strategic, operational, tactical or project levels. Both standards clearly evoke the dynamic and variable nature of human behavior and risk-aware culture and should be considered throughout this process.[1] Let's begin with information on ISO 31000:2018 (see Figure 5.1). Later in the chapter, we will look at the risk management process using the perspective of COSO ERM:2017.

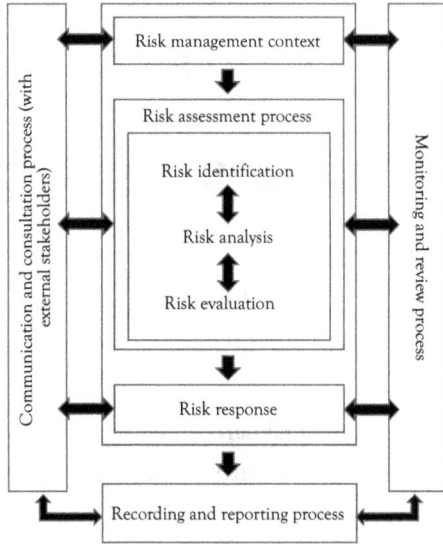

Figure 5.1 ISO 31000 risk management process[2]

Communication and Consultation

Unlike other risk management standards in use today, ISO 31000:2018 requires the organization to seek involvement of external stakeholders within the communication and consultation process. These are the same external stakeholders that are engaged with during a PESTLE scan of the external operating environment. The stakeholders identified in that process can participate in risk assessment and other activities in this risk management process to examine opportunities and threats found in the scan. Open two-way, face-to-face communication over the long term is exactly what works to improve the ability to receive feedback and information that will be used in decision making. These efforts happen even with protection of confidentiality and integrity of the information as well as the privacy rights of individuals. The success of many of the early stakeholder engagements has provided the lessons-learned to advance the stakeholder engagement process and develop the set of skills in organizations that can most benefit from this exchange with the stakeholders. Communication and consultation with external and internal stakeholders should take place within and throughout ALL steps of the risk management process.[3]

Here are some of the means by which communication can be successful within the risk management process[4]:

- Bring different areas of expertise together for each step of the iterative risk management process.
- Ensure that different views are appropriately considered when defining risks criteria and when evaluating risk.
- Enable the organization to calibrate its risk appetite.
- Prevent assumptions and prejudices about potential risks and controls from interfering with their consideration and discussion.
- Provides enough information to facilitate risk oversight and decision making.
- Builds a sense of inclusiveness and ownership among those stakeholders affected by risk.

Monitoring and Review

A similar effort to communications is the monitoring and review process. The purpose of this effort is to assure and improve the quality and effectiveness of process design, implementation and outcomes. "Monitoring and review" does so by providing ongoing monitoring and periodic review of the risk management process.

Monitoring and review take place at all stages of the process—before, during and at the end of the iterative steps described as being part of the process. This effort should include planning, gathering and analyzing information, recording results and providing feedback to the people involved in the process, including the communication and consultation efforts. The results of monitoring and review should be incorporated throughout the organization's performance management, measurement and reporting activities.[5]

Recording and Reporting

This is the third process providing a level of oversight on the risk management process. People involved in this activity oversee documentation and reporting of the risk management process. Here are examples of what is accomplished within recording and reporting[6]:

- Communication of risk management activities and outcomes across the organization
- Provides information for decision making
- Continually improves risk management activities
- Assists interaction with stakeholders and those with responsibility and accountability for risk management activities
- Defines the use of the information including the sensitivity of that information
- Provides important input to management for decisions on the creation retention and handling of documented information

Reporting is an integral part of an organization's governance and should enhance the quality of the engagement with stakeholders and support the top company leader in meeting their accountability obligations for risk management.

Risk Management Process

The risk management process is where risk assessment is performed. Risk assessment has several supporting tasks that are important to provide a context to risk assessment and to enable its findings to be incorporated into the risk response.

Establishing the Risk Management Context

The risk management context is articulated at the start of the risk management process. While it is different than the organization's internal and external context, it does require that people involved in the process of risk management understand the external and internal contexts and how they are changing. The external and internal contexts are described in Chapter 1. They help the risk manager identify the opportunities and threats found in the scanning of the internal and external operating environments of the organization. The risk management context then defines the specific environment of the activity to which the risk management process is to be applied.[7]

Understanding the risk management context is important because[8]:

- Risk management addresses the "effects of uncertainty" (opportunities and threats) on the ability of the organization to meet its objectives.
- Organizational factors can be a source of risk in addition to the opportunities and threats.
- The purpose and scope of where the risk management process is being applied can be interrelated with the objectives of the organization.

The organization should specify the amount and type of risk that it may or may not take relative to its objectives. It is referred to as its risk appetite (see Chapter 6). The organization should also define criteria to evaluate the significance of risk and to support decision-making processes. Risk criteria should be aligned with the risk management framework (see Chapter 4) and customized to a specific purpose and scope of the activity under consideration. Risk criteria should reflect the organization's values, objectives, and resources and be consistent with policies and statements about risk management. These criteria should be defined considering the organization's obligations and engagement with stakeholders.[9]

Risk Assessment

Risk assessment includes risk identification, risk analysis and risk evaluation. Risk assessment should be conducted systematically, iteratively and collaboratively, drawing on engagement with stakeholders through communication and consultation activity.

Risk identification is used to find, recognize and describe risks (both opportunities and threats) that might help or prevent an organization from achieving its strategic objectives (see Chapter 1). The organization should identify opportunities and threats, whether their sources are under its control (e.g., internal versus external context risks). These risks are expressed as the effects of uncertainty—opportunities and threats. Remember that pure risks (hazards and loss risks) will be handled through risk control procedures, not the risk management program. These two programs are kept separate because pure risk is insurable, and the risks derived from the "effects of uncertainty" are not insurable and do not contribute to the total cost of insurance.

Risk analysis helps to understand the nature of risk and its characteristics. It involves a detailed consideration of uncertainties, risk sources, consequences of the risk, likelihood of the risk, events, and scenarios. Risk analysis can be conducted with varying degrees of detail and formality, depending on the purpose of the analysis, the availability and reliability of information, and the resources available. Analysis techniques can be qualitative, semiquantitative, quantitative or a combination of these, depending on the circumstances and intended use of the information.[10]

Risk analysis is usually determined using likelihood and consequence determinations. The consequences are negative for threats and positive for opportunities. The likelihood is always positive. This provides a means of using a risk map (see Figure 5.2) that plots the opportunities on the right and the threats on the left. In this way, the organization can select an opportunity that would appear to be able to offset some of the high-scoring threats on the left side of the heat diagram.

Risk analysis can be influenced by opinions, biases, perceptions of risk and judgments of those associated with the risk management process. Additional influences are the quality of the information used, assumptions and exclusions made, any limitations of techniques, and how they are executed. These influences need to be considered in the communication and consultation process as well as the monitoring and review process. The results provide insight for decisions, where choices are being made, and the options involve different types and levels of risk.[11]

Risk evaluation is conducted to support decisions. Risks evaluation involves comparing results of the risk analysis with established risk criteria to determine the significance of risk. This can lead to a decision to:

- Do nothing further.
- Consider risk response options.
- Undertake further analysis to better understand risk.
- Maintain existing hazard controls.
- Reconsider the objectives.
- Eliminate the risk altogether by avoiding the activity creating the risk.

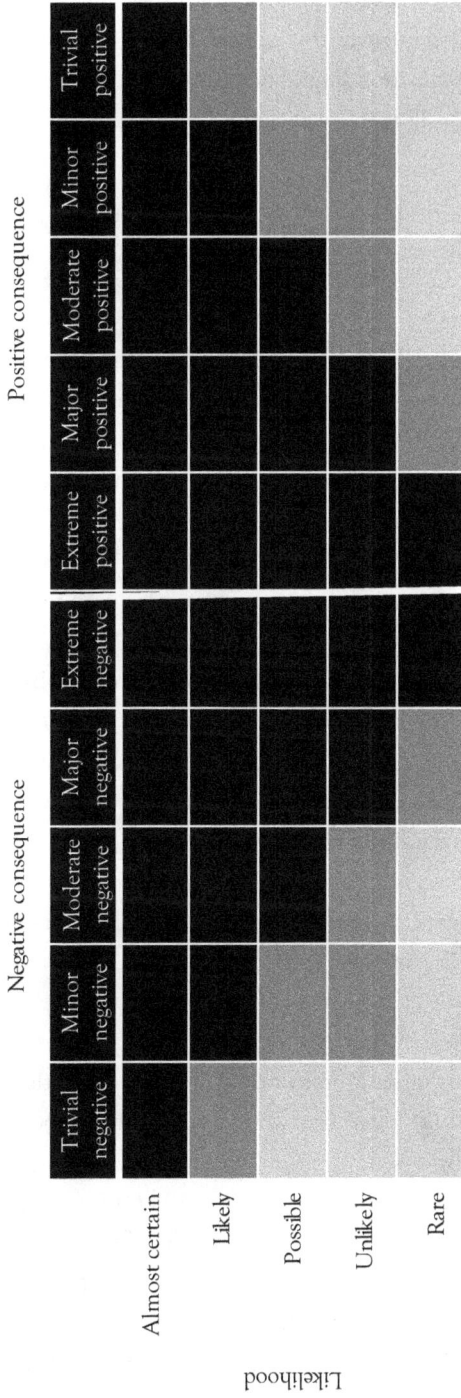

Figure 5.2 Risk matrix for the risk analysis[12]

Decisions should take account of the wider context as well as actual and perceived consequences for external and internal stakeholders. The outcome of risk evaluation should be subject to communication and consultation, monitoring and review and recording and reporting.

Risk Response

The purpose of risk response (the term used in COSO ERM:2017) is to select and implement responses for addressing risk. Some risk identification teams focus only on threats even though it is clear that "effects of uncertainty" include both opportunities and threats. Typically, response involves exploiting significant opportunities while trying to offset major threats. In some organizations, lowering the impact of the threats is referred to as "risk treatment." There are many tools available to treat threats. They are presented in ISO 31010:2009.[13] However, it is important to know that many of these tools can also be used to characterize the best process for dealing with the opportunities.

What would happen if the opportunity is exploited by the risk manager but does not yield a diminished risk level as a result of that process? The constraint to developing opportunities as a response is solely a function of an organization's experience and comfort developing opportunities. To optimize the risk response, an evaluation of opportunities assists in making decisions on the response based the analysis of the opportunities described earlier. The generic strategy for uncertainty evaluation consists of the following four steps[14]:

- *Eliminate uncertainty*: Seek to remove threats or offset threats with opportunities, remembering that opportunities have risk associated with them should they not be able to be exploited successfully.
- *Allocate ownership*: Seek to either transfer uncertainty to a third party to share in the effect of a loss for a fee, or transfer ownership of an opportunity to a third party that can maximize benefit with a payment to the organization.
- *Modify exposure*: In the management of threats, this is referred to as mitigation, an attempt to reduce likelihood or

consequences. When an opportunity is successfully implemented, thereby removing its threat to the organization, the
outcome is on the upside of risk, thereby avoiding the need to
mitigate a threat.

- *Include in the baseline*: Opportunities and threats that are not
significant as a result of the analysis can be put on a "watch
list" to monitor if changes occur to make them more significant uncertainties. It is important to consider multiple opportunities and threats that alone would end up in the baseline,
but when clustered may need some other form of response.

You can also look at these four evaluation categories from the perspective of threats[15]:

- *Avoid*: Seek to remove threats to lower or eliminate
uncertainty.
- *Transfer*: Allocate ownership to enable effective management
of a threat, often using an insurance company or contractual
terms and conditions for this purpose.
- *Mitigate*: Reduce the likelihood or consequence of the threat
below an acceptable threshold.
- *Accept:* Recognize residual risks associated with uncertainty
and devise ways to control or monitor them.

There are four major categories of controls that can be used for
opportunities[16]:

- *Exploit* identified opportunities, removing or reducing uncertainty by seeking to make the opportunity succeed.
- *Enhance* means increasing its positive likelihood or consequence to maximize the benefit of the opportunity.
- *Share* opportunities by passing ownership to a third party best
able to manage the opportunity and maximize the chance of
it happening.
- *Ignore* opportunities adopting a reactive approach without
taking explicit actions.

COSO ERM:2017 Approach to the Risk Management Process

COSO ERM:2017 applies a series of "principles" to gauge performance of the process instead of presenting this activity as a management system process. This performance component will be discussed here for the reader to be able to see the differences.

Principles Relating to Performance

Organizations seek to meet their strategic objectives in an uncertain world. They seek to identify, assess and respond to risk as the means for accomplishing this most important task. Risk management becomes the preferred means for addressing performance in the COSO ERM:2017 standard. As stated at the top of this chapter, there are five "principles" that support the organization in making decisions and supporting objectives. Organizations use the COSO ERM:2017 operating structure to develop a performance enhanced practice that[17]:

- Identifies new and emerging risks so that leadership can deploy risk responses in a timely manner.
- Assesses the severity of risk, with an understanding of how the risk may change depending on the level within the organization (strategic, operational, or tactical).
- Prioritizes risks, allowing management to optimize allocation of resources in response to those risks.
- Identifies and selects responses to risk.
- If the organization is a corporation, develop a portfolio view to enhance the ability to articulate the amount of risks assumed in the pursuit of meeting its strategic objectives.

Identifies Risk (Principle 10)

Every organization must identify internal and external context risks that can impact its drive to meet its strategic objectives. The organization undertakes risk identification activities to first establish an inventory of risks, and to confirm existing risks. Knowledge and awareness of risks needs to be maintained as part of how the organization operates every day. It is a good idea to periodically test the completeness of the risks inventory.[18]

COSO ERM:2017 provides information on how to develop and use a risk inventory and a discussion of approaches to identifying risk given the differences that might exist from facility to facility. The COSO ERM:2017 section ends with a review on how best to frame risk by focusing on the upside (a potential gain) or downside (a potential loss).[19]

Assesses Severity of Risk (Principle 11)

Risks identified and included in the risks inventory are assessed in order to understand the severity of each to the organization's ability to meet its strategic objectives. Risk assessments inform the selection of risk responses. Given the severity of risks identified, management must decide on the resources and capabilities to deploy for the risks to remain within the organization's risk appetite.

COSO ERM:2017 provides information on the following topics[20]:

- Assessing severity at different levels of the organization
- Selecting severity measures
- Assessment approaches: qualitative, quantitative or a combination of both
- Differentiating between inherent, target and residual risk
- Depicting assessment risk assessment results
- Identifying "triggers" for reassessment
- Dealing with bias in risk assessment

Prioritizes Risks (Principle 12)

The risks assessed in the previous principle are prioritized by the organization as a basis for selecting responses. This task is described in these sections[21]:

- Establishing the criteria
- Prioritizing the risks—general considerations
- Using the risk appetite to prioritize risks

- Prioritizing risks at all levels in the organization
- Dealing with bias in the prioritization effort

Implementing the Risk Responses (Principle 13)

The organization now must identify and select risk responses. The following sections provide details on how the implementation is conducted[22]:

- Factors for choosing the risk responses
- Selecting and deploying risk responses
- Considering costs and benefits of risk responses
- Additional considerations

Developing a Portfolio View of Risk

This is a specialized area of risk management that helps risk managers consider potential implications to the risk profile from an entity-wide or portfolio perspective. A portfolio view allows management and the board to consider the type, severity, and interdependencies of risks and how they may affect performance. Using a portfolio view, the organization can identify risks that are severe at the corporate level. This is the key difference between risk management and enterprise risk management.

Integrating ISO 31000:2018 and COSO ERM:2017

The ISO 31000:2018 risk management system is just 16 pages long as compared to the 110 pages in COSO ERM 2017. Given the brevity of ISO 31000:2018, the leader of the organization and others involved must supplement the ISO 31000:2018 information with the supporting information found in the Australian guidance. Fortunately, there were not many changes between the two documents (2009 version vs. the 2018 version). Due to the large changes involved in the COSO ERM 2017 update, the risk assessment activities are now quite like those found in ISO 31000:2018. The risk management team should be able to put together an integrated document that meets the needs of the organization and its leaders. Figure 5.3 provides the framework for COSO ERM: 2017.[23]

| Governance and culture |
| Information, communication and reporting |

| Mission, vision and core values | Strategy development | Business objective formulation | Implementation and performance | Enhance value |

| Strategy and objective-setting |
| Performance |
| Review and revision |

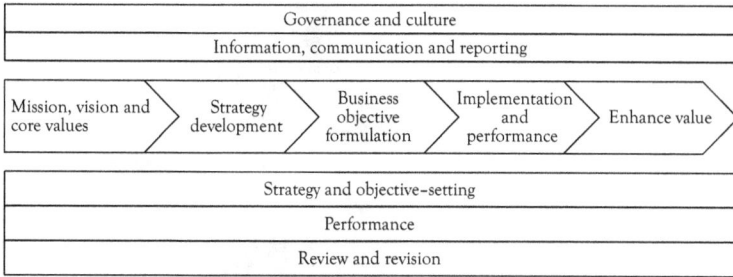

Figure 5.3 COSO ERM:2017 process[24]

Chapter 6 will present a case for 'giving effect' to the integrated risk management systems that allow the organization to include other items that are important to their organization.

Notes

1. ISO (2018).
2. ISO (2018).
3. ISO (2018).
4. ISO (2018).
5. ISO (2018).
6. ISO (2018).
7. ISO (2018).
8. ISO (2018).
9. ISO (2018).
10. Pojasek (2017).
11. ISO (2018).
12. Pojasek (2017).
13. ISO (2009).
14. Pojasek (2017).
15. Pojasek (2017).
16. Pojasek (2017).
17. COSO (2017).
18. COSO (2017).
19. COSO (2017).
20. COSO (2017).
21. COSO (2017).
22. COSO (2017).
23. COSO (2017).
24. COSO (2017).

CHAPTER 6

COSO ERM:2017
Contributions

Introduction

Previous chapters presented numerous examples of how (International Organization for Standardization) ISO and COSO risk management standards work in a collaborative manner. In this chapter, we will explore some of the "principles" in COSO ERM:2017 that can be added to ISO 31000:2018 to improve risk management effectiveness.

By having a focus on an "enterprise risk management" program, COSO ERM:2017 helps people manage financial risks and compliance with the provisions of Sarbanes-Oxley Section 401. It also can help improve the management of "non-financial" risks associated with issues such as fraud and cybercrimes. Some companies use ISO 31000:2018 for the non-financial risks and COSO ERM:2017 for the financial risks. Each standard can handle both financial and non-financial risks, however, integrating both into the organization's risk management program is better than only using one.

This chapter will highlight the business value that is found in COSO ERM:2017 and how it can contribute to the International risk management system standard, ISO 31000:2018.

Enhanced Value Model

In ISO 31000:2018, risk is defined as the "effects of uncertainty" and how they affect the ability of an organization to meet its strategic objectives. There is a model that shows how an organization derives its strategic objectives from the mission statement[1] (see Figure 6.1). It is a model that is commonly found in the organizational development field.

Mission   Create value

O   O   O

Strategic objectives

| Mission, vision, core values | Strategy development | Formulate objectives | Perform | Enhanced value |

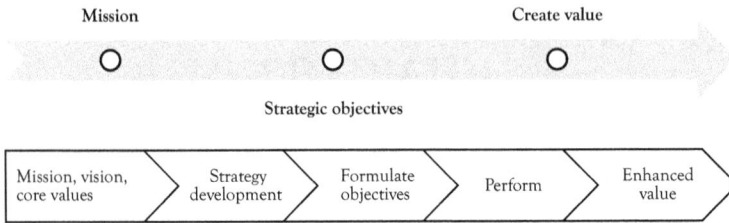

Figure 6.1 *Difference between ISO 31000 (top) and COSO ERM (Bottom)*

COSO ERM:2017 has developed a more robust model (referred to as an ERM framework—not to be confused with the ISO 31000:2018 risk management framework for an organization to seek enhanced value (Figure 6.1). COSO ERM:2017 provides a five-step process as compared to the three-step process associated with ISO 31000:2018. The sequence of mission statement, objectives, and value are found in both models.

There are five "components" supporting this enterprise risk management model[2]:

1. Governance and Culture
2. Strategy and Objective-Setting
3. Performance
4. Review and Revision
5. Information, Communication, and Reporting

Each of these components in COSO ERM:2017 contain principles. A number of these principles have been presented in previous chapters. In this chapter, the focus will be on components 2, 4 and 5 as listed in the preceding five "components."

Strategy and Objective Setting Component

Organizations use strategy to make sure that their mission and strategic objectives are achieved. This process creates what strategists call "enhanced value." Strategy is practiced in an implicit or explicit manner. However, it must be carefully aligned with risk management to be effective. By integrating strategy-setting with risk management, an organization can gain insight into the risk profile associated with business objectives and strategy. This activity is valuable because it guides the organization to take steps necessary to move from the mission statement to the best value-building outcomes.[3]

There are four principles in this component:

- Analyze Business Context
- Define Risk Appetite
- Evaluate Alternative Strategies
- Formulate Business Objectives

Analyzes Business Context

The ISO 31000:2018 use of context is explained in Chapter 1. Every organization should consider its organization's internal and external context when developing strategy to support its value creation process as described earlier. COSO ERM:2017 views context as trends, relationships and other factors that influence an organization's current and future strategy and business objectives. This view complements the risk identification process in the ISO 31000:2018 risk management process. Although context is a key element in the ISO "high-level structure" for all of its management system standards, functional managers rarely wish to pursue risk management associated with external context factors. Their focus is on the internal context where they have more control of risks. The top leaders must make sure that the context information is used as an important element in the risk management process.

Defines Risk Appetite

Risk appetite is defined as the "types and amount of risk, on a board or top leader level, and organization is willing to accept in pursuit of value.[4]" There is no standard for "risk appetite." Setting risk appetite is commonly done in corporations though the board of directors' governance structure. But it can be used more informally to help smaller organizations specify the acceptable types and amounts of risk. COSO ERM:2017 provides detailed information for organizations in each of these areas:

- Applying risk appetite concept
- Determining risk appetite
- Articulating risk appetite
- Using risk appetite

Chapter 3 in this book addresses how the organization's principles are developed to support the risk-aware culture.

Evaluates Alternative Strategies

In COSO ERM:2017, strategy is defined as "the organization's plan to achieve its mission" (as expressed by its strategic objectives, vision, and core values). All organizations should create and evaluate alternative strategies as part of strategy development and assess the opportunities and threats of each option. Alternative strategies are assessed in the context of the organization's resources and capabilities to create, preserve, and realize value. The strategy needs to support mission and vision and align with the core values and risk appetite. If it does not align, an organization may not achieve its strategic objectives.

There are several important steps that need to be included in the evaluation of alternative strategies[5]:

- Knowing the importance of aligning strategy with risk management
- Understanding the implications from the chosen strategy
- Aligning strategy with risk appetite
- Making changes to strategy
- Mitigating bias in the strategy process

Formulates Business Objectives

COSO ERM:2017 defines business objectives as "those measurable steps the organization takes to achieve its strategy.[6]" While this works well for publicly traded companies with a board of directors, most organizations, whether they have a board or not, seek to meet their "objectives" in an uncertain world. Strategy provides a good guide to make sure organizations consider risk and strategy at all levels that align and support strategy.

It is prudent to follow the ISO 31000:2018 information on organizations while also considering advice of COSO ERM:2017. The following guidance on formulating business objectives is available in COSO ERM:2017:

- Establishing business objectives
- Aligning business objectives
- Understanding the implications from chosen business objectives
- Categorizing business objectives
- Setting performance measures and targets
- Understanding tolerance
- Performance measures and established tolerances

Review and Revisions Component

An organization's strategy, objectives and risk management practices, and capabilities may change as it adapts to uncertainty found in its internal and external context. These changes result in current risk management practices no longer applying or being sufficient to support achievement of current or updated objectives. When necessary, the organization should revise the practices, especially the risk management efforts. There are three principles that pertain to this practice.[7]

Assess Substantial Change

Organizations need to identify and asses changes that may substantially affect strategy and objectives. Changes take place in the internal and external operating environments. These should be considered within the setting of strategy and articulation of objectives at all levels of the organization. However, the organization must remain aware of the potential for larger, substantial changes that may occur and have a more pronounced effect on its ability to meet its objectives. Substantial change may lead to new or changed risks and affect key assumptions that support the strategy and the setting of the objectives. Practices for identifying such changes should be built into risk management program efforts. This principle provides useful examples of substantial change in both the internal and external environment. This information is useful to organization leaders to help fulfill the accountability for meeting the objectives of the organization.[8]

Review Risk and Performance

Organization leaders are expected to review performance and consider risk. This is consistent with the responsibilities and accountability within risk management oversight. The purpose of this activity is to reduce the type and amount of risk to acceptable levels and to pursuing new opportunities as they emerge. From time to time, organizations may need to assess its risk management capabilities and practices. By continually reviewing performance, organizations can seek answers to questions such as[9]:

- Has the entity performed as expected and achieved its objectives?
- What risks are occurring that may be affecting performance?
- Was the organization taking enough risk to attain its target?
- Was the estimate of the amount of risk accurate?

If an organization determines that performance does not fall within its acceptable variation, it may need to[10]:

- Review objectives and all levels of the organization
- Review strategy
- Review the organization's risk-aware culture
- Revise performance levels
- Reassess severity of risk results
- Review how risks are prioritized
- Revise risk responses
- Revise risk appetite

The extent of any corrective actions should align with magnitude of deviations in performance. Additionally, an organization may need to consider its capabilities and their effects on performance.

Pursues Improvement in Risk Management

Organizations must pursue continual improvement of its risk management capability. Even those organizations with enough risk management activity can become more effective. By embedding continual evaluations by management review into business practices, organizations can systematically identify potential improvements to their enterprise risk management practices. Opportunities to review and improve efficiency and effectiveness should consider the following areas[11]:

- Management of change
- New technologies
- Historical shortcomings
- Risk appetite
- Risk identification
- Internal communication
- Stakeholder engagement
- Benchmarking results
- Rate of change

Information, Communications and Reporting Component

Advances in technology and business use of digital methods have resulted in exponential growth in amount, use and speed which data must be processed, organized, and stored. It is important that organizations provide the right information, in the right form, at the right level of detail, to the right people, at the right time[12]!

Organizations transform data into information about stakeholder engagement, products, markets, and competitor activities. Through available communication channels, organizations can provide timely, relevant information to targeted audiences. This information helps organizations identify risks. This information also facilitates decision making and provides a competitive advantage.

Leverage Information and Technology

Organizations must leverage its information and technology systems to support risk management. Organizations also use information to anticipate situations that may prevent them from meeting their objectives. There is information for governance, risk-aware culture, strategy, objective setting, performance-related practices, as well as for review and revision-related practices. COSO ERM:2017 provides useful information on each of the following topics[13]:

- Putting relevant information to use
- Managing evolving information
- Categorizing risk information
- Managing data
- Using technology to support information
- Changing requirements

Communicates Risk Information

Channels are available to the organization for communicating risk data and information to internal and external stakeholders. These channels enable organizations to provide information for use in decision making.[14] This COSO ERM:2017 section contains a listing of communication channels that enable management to convey relevant information. In addition, this section explains how to communicate with the board or top leader. This is useful for comparison to what you may be doing now in your own organization.

Reports on Risk, Culture, and Performance

Reporting supports people at all levels in an organization to understand relationships between risk, culture, and performance and to improve decision making in strategy and objective setting, governance, and day-to-day operations. Among the topics covered in this principle are[15]:

- Identifying report users and their roles
- Reporting attributes
- Types of reporting
- Reporting risk to the board
- Reporting on risk-aware culture

- Key indicators
- Reporting frequency and quality

A Call for Integration of ISO 31000:2018 and COSO:2017

Any organization seeking to implement or improve an existing risk management program should consider guidance provided in both ISO 31000:2018 and COSO:2017. Remember that ISO 31000:2018 has a useful supporting document[16] to provide the level of detail to that standard as the COSO ERM:2017 delivers.

In the final chapter of this book, you will be provided information on how to best integrate this information and make it available to everyone that is involved in the risk management effort. This will complete your leader's view on this topic.

Notes

1. ISO (2014).
2. COSO (2017).
3. COSO (2017).
4. COSO (2017).
5. COSO (2017).
6. COSO (2017).
7. COSO (2017).
8. COSO (2017).
9. COSO (2017).
10. COSO (2017).
11. COSO (2017).
12. COSO (2017).
13. COSO (2017).
14. COSO ERM (2017).
15. COSO (2017).
16. Standards Australia and Standards New Zealand (2013).

CHAPTER 7

Integrating Risk Management into the Organization

Introduction

Risk management is the focus of information presented in the first six chapters of this book. Two recently-updated risk management systems are presented, ISO 31000:2018 and COSO ERM:2017. These standards can be integrated for more effective use. However, risk management could be even more effective if it were additionally integrated into how business is operated every day.

The International Organization for Standardization (ISO) created a "high-level structure" (HLS) that is used to write and integrate management system standards and enable them to work more effectively as a part of the business. With a HLS in place, an organization can use "Software-as-a-Service" (SaaS) as a tool to manage the risk program and to facilitate its interaction with other functions within the organization. The HLS has been approved by over 180 national standardization organizations.

ISO defines a management system as a set of procedures an organization needs to follow in order to meet its objectives. Risk is the effects of uncertainty on the ability of an organization to meet its objectives. Instead of separating risk management on its own, it is important to use it across all organization activities. This will align the principles of risk management and the risk-based culture that is described in Chapter 3.

ISO High Level Structure

The HLS is publicly available as the ISO/IEC Directives Part 1[1] (Annex SL, Appendix 2). A figure shows the content of the HLS[2] (Figure 7.1). This framework provides a generic management system intended to be

Scope
Normative Reference
Terms and Definitions
Context of the Organization
    Understanding the Organization and its Context
    Understanding the Interests of the Stakeholders
    Determining the Scope of the Integrated Management System
    Integrated Management System
Leadership
    Leadership and Commitment
    Policy
    Organizational Roles, Responsibilities and Authorities
Planning
    Actions to Address Risk—Opportunities and Threats
    Integrated Management System Objectives and Planning to Achieve Them
Support
    Resources
    Competence
    Awareness
    Communication
    Documented Information
        General
        Creating and Updating
        Control of Documented Information
Operation
    Operational Planning and Control
Performance Evaluation
    Monitoring, Measurement, Analysis, and Evaluation
    Internal Audit
        Conduct Internal Audits
        Internal Audit Program
    Management Review
Improvement
    Improvement and Corrective Action
    Continual Improvement

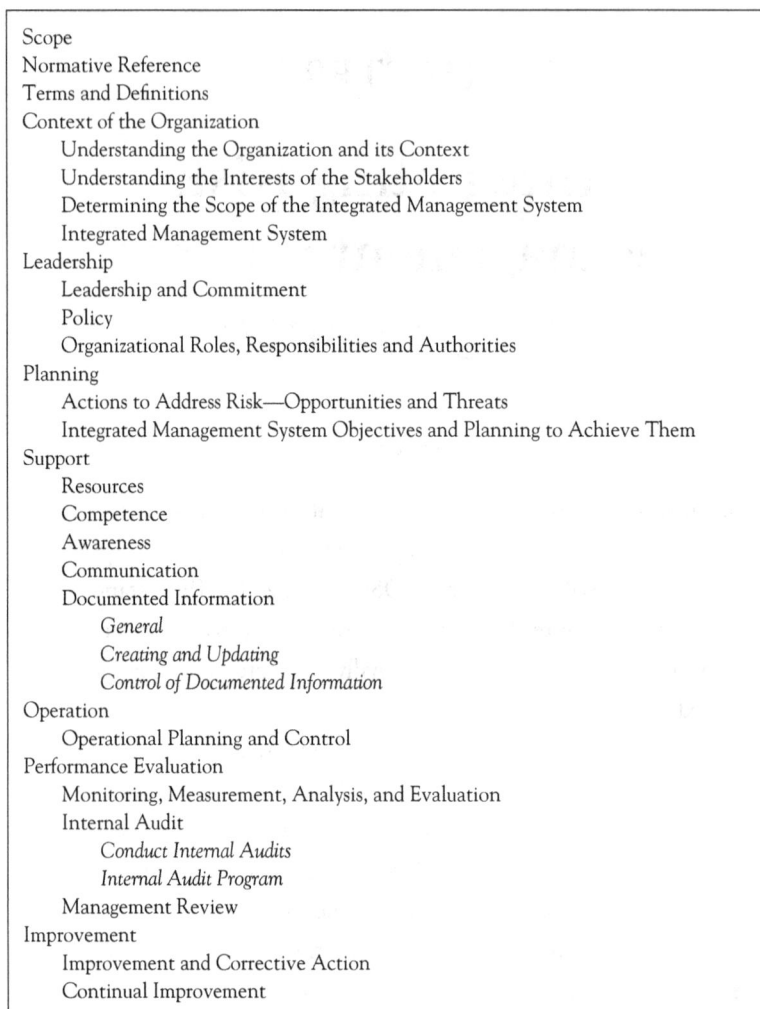

Figure 7.1 ISO high-level structure[3]

a blueprint for all new and revised ISO management system standards going forward. This generic framework is to be expanded to address specific needs and different industry types. The following sections provide more information about the elements of the HLS.

Context of the Organization

Context is used to introduce risk management directly into the HLS. This enables the organization to specify requirements for a strategic understanding of important issues that can affect its ability to meet its objectives within the organization's operations management system. These issues can be expressed as opportunities and threats and the effects on the organization can be positive or negative.

An organization must also understand the interests of its internal and external stakeholders regarding operation of the organization. Some of these interests may become requirements of the organization if it voluntarily decides to adopt them. Other interests are either not relevant to the organization's management system or are mandatory because they have been incorporated into laws, regulations, permits, and licenses by governmental or court action. Any of these interests that are adopted by the organization become organizational requirements and may be monitored closely by the engagement of its stakeholders.

Organizations determine the scope of the management system to establish physical and organizational boundaries to which the management system will apply. An understanding of the context and interests of its stakeholders are major considerations when establishing the scope of the management system and in determining which requirements the organization will adopt. Documentation of the scope is created and controlled in accordance with the requirements of the document information capability.

The intent of the management system is to specify overarching requirement(s) related to creating the "necessary but sufficient" set of processes that form an effective operation. Each organization retains authority, accountability, and autonomy, to decide how it will fulfill those requirements, including the level of detail and extent to which it will integrate the requirements into its business.

Leadership and Commitment

The intent of leadership and commitment is to demonstrate actions in which top management is personally involved with and directs in the organization. Certainly, top management may not perform all these actions themselves, but they are accountable for making sure the actions are performed. Furthermore, top management is held directly accountable for the objectives established in the management system.

A management system must be integrated into the organization's business processes. This is what binds the management system to what people in the organization do every day. The responsibility for this integration into business processes (i.e., not operating as a "stand-alone" management system) is emphasized in the management system and is assigned as one of the top manager's roles.

Top management is required to create a culture and environment that encourages people with leadership roles to work actively toward implementing requirements of the management system and achieve the objectives.

A policy is developed and used to specify the high-level organizational commitments required of each operational area found in the integrated management system, considering the organization's purpose. It is used to frame objectives which the organization sets for itself in each management system included in the integrated management system. The policy is documented and communicated internally in accordance with the management system's communications specifications. This policy is also made available to external stakeholders to guide them in the engagement process.

Planning

Planning is the first element of the "plan-do-check-act" (PDCA) operating structure. The context and leadership are considered "pre-planning" activities that will be useful for framing the PDCA efforts. The requirements for planning are needed as a prerequisite to establishing the management system.

This planning activity in the PDCA sequence opens with a section to deal with "potential adverse effects (threats) and potential beneficial effects (opportunities)" that are identified in the work to scan the internal and external context and efforts to engage with the stakeholders. It is important to avoid the term "risks and opportunities" because uncertainty risk cannot be used as a synonym for threats.

Planning is performed at a strategic level. At a minimum, planning needs to consider the issues relevant to the organization's context (as discussed in Chapter 1) in order to address any negative or positive consequence in a prioritized fashion. Prioritization is based on the following items:

- Assure the integrated management system can achieve its intended outcome(s)

- Prevent, or reduce, undesired effects of uncertainty
- Achieve continual improvement

In most cases the integrated management systems need to use both a risk management approach and risk response approach.

The purpose of planning is to anticipate potential scenarios and consequences to help prevent undesired effects before they occur. Similarly, planning looks for favorable conditions or circumstances that can offer a potential advantage or beneficial outcome worthy of pursuit.

Planning also includes determining how to incorporate actions deemed necessary or beneficial into the integrated management system, either through objective setting, operational control, resource provision, competence, or other specific elements found in the management system. The mechanism for evaluating the effectiveness of benefiting from the opportunities (i.e., preventive actions) can include monitoring and measurement techniques, internal audit, or management review.

An organization will specify objectives in each management system area (e.g., environment, health and safety, energy management, business continuity planning) that are linked to the policy, leadership and commitment. Objectives should be specified in a way that allows determination of their fulfillment to be made by monitoring, measurement, analysis, and evaluation and updated as appropriate, consistent with continual improvement. Objectives are communicated in accordance with the communications activities. Documentation of objectives is created and controlled in accordance with the requirements of documented information.

Actions required to achieve objectives and associated timeframe are determined. In addition, assignment of responsibility for doing it is established in accordance with requirements of organization roles, responsibilities and authorities. Any need for budgets, specialized skills, technology or infrastructure are determined in accordance with the requirements of monitoring, measurement, analysis and evaluation and reported within the management review.

Support Functions

The HLS pays attention to the level of support required for the PDCA sequence that is commonly underemphasized in management systems. This includes the following:

- Resources
- Competence
- Awareness
- Communication
- Documented information

What is involved in conforming to each of these functions is presented in the HLS. How the organization conforms to these areas is determined by the organization.

Operational Planning and Control

This section of the integrated management system specifies requirements that need to be implemented within the organization's operations to make sure the integrated management system requirements are fulfilled, and the priority opportunities and threats are being addressed.

Operational control includes the methods implemented to make sure business operations, activities or equipment do not exceed specified conditions or performance standards or violate regulatory compliance limits. This is in line with the achievement of the intended outcomes of the management system(s). These controls help meet technical specifications, operating parameters, or a prescribed methodology.

Operational control is required for situations related to business processes where absence of controls could lead to deviations from the policy and objectives or poses unacceptable risk. These situations can be related to business operations, activities or processes production, installation or servicing, maintenance, or contractors, suppliers or vendors. The degree of control exercised will vary depending on many factors, including functions performed, their importance or complexity, potential consequences of deviation or variability or the technical competency involved versus what is available.

Requirements for "management of change," both planned and unintended changes, are required to prevent or otherwise minimize the chance technical requirements are not fulfilled, or new risks are introduced. When operational controls fail, action is necessary to address any resultant undesired effect(s).

Performance Evaluation

The intent of monitoring, measurement, analysis, and evaluation is to specify requirements for implementing checks to be sure the intended results of the integrated management system are achieved. Checking can be qualitative (monitoring) or quantitative (measurement). The organization determines:

- What needs to be monitored and measured.
- The methods for monitoring, measurement, analysis and evaluation, as applicable to ensure valid results.
- When the results from monitoring and measurement need to be analyzed and evaluated.

The characteristics that are monitored or measured, analyzed and evaluated provide information to judge the extent to which the integrated management system planned activities are realized and its planned results are achieved. The information gathered from monitoring or measurement, analysis and evaluation is presented to top management as part of the management review. Documentation of the monitoring, measurement, analysis and evaluation results is created and controlled in accordance with requirements of the documented information.

The organization should maintain a program of internal or external audits to check that the management system conforms to both written requirements and any requirements the organization self imposes. The audits also need to determine that the management system is being effectively implemented and maintained as planned.

An audit program requires that:

- Internal audits be planned and scheduled based on the importance of the processes audited and the results of previous audits.
- A methodology for planning and conducting internal audits needs to be established.
- The roles and responsibilities within the audit program must be assigned, considering the integrity and independence of the internal audit process.

- The audit criteria (i.e., policies, procedures or requirements used as a reference against which relevant and verifiable records, statements of fact or other information will be compared) and audit scope (i.e., description of the physical locations, organizational units, activities and processes, as well as the time period covered) for each audit planned.

The audit program is planned and implemented and maintained by internal personnel or can be managed by external persons acting on the organization's behalf. In either case, the selection of audit program personnel needs to meet competence requirements.

Management systems require a holistic review of the management system on a periodic basis by the top management team. Usually the management review is scheduled for a quarterly or semi-annual meeting. Like a board of directors, the management review can set up more frequent reviews of specific sections of the management system and report back to the entire management review at the designated time. Over the long haul, this has been the one element of international management system standards that has added the most value to the continual improvement cycle.

Top management is required to be personally engaged in this review. It is their responsibility to drive changes to the management system and direct continual improvement priorities, particularly in relation to the changing circumstances in the organization's context, deviations from intended results, or favorable conditions that offer an advantage with beneficial outcomes. As with most of the other sections mentioned earlier, documentation is required for all the activities of the management review team.

Improvement

This final section of the management system HLS specifies requirements for responding when the management system standard requirements are not satisfied. One of the requirements of this section is for what is referred to as nonconformity and corrective action. This section of the management system requires taking action to correct the situation, examines causes for the situation and determine if other occurrences exist or potentially exist elsewhere so that action can be taken to prevent reoccurrence. Further, it requires evaluation of the action taken to confirm that the intended result was achieved and evaluation of the management system to determine if changes are warranted to avoid future occurrences of similar nonconformities.

Continual improvement specifies the requirements to improve the management system. Improvement is focused generally in four areas:

- Suitability—the extent to which the management system fits and is right for the organization's purpose, its operations, culture, and business systems.
- Adequacy—the extent to which the management system is sufficient in meeting the applicable requirements.
- Effectiveness—the extent to which planned activities are realized and planned results achieved.
- Timeliness—in anomalous or urgent situations, delay in response could be costly and potentially hazardous; delay in critical items may be consequential.

Continual improvement involves making changes to the design and implementation of the management system in order to improve the organization's ability to achieve conformity with the requirements of the management system and meet its objectives and policy commitments. Although there may be value in improving the system elements alone, the intended outcome of planned actions and other management system changes is an improvement in the organization's performance. A coordinated implementation of the integrated management system may help to develop a robust way to achieve this improvement, including the following:

- Taking actions to address risk (opportunities and threats)
- Establishing objectives for each of the management systems included in the integrated management system to provide a means of measuring progress on the strategic objectives
- Upgrading operational controls taking into consideration new technologies, methods or information
- Analyzing and evaluating performance
- Conducting internal audits

- Conducting management system reviews by organization leaders
- Detecting nonconformity(ies) and implementing corrective actions.

Integration of Risk Management

The HLS introduces contextual risk into the management system structure. This is how the organization will find opportunities and threats. At the same time, the scanning of the internal and external operating environment becomes part of each of the management systems that can be integrated and used to guide the operations of the organization.

In the planning section the opportunities and threats are examined using risk assessment to help create the objectives for each of the management systems that are put into play within the organization. These objectives are carefully aligned with the strategic objectives that are derived from the mission statement.

Something as important as risk management should not be conducted independently of how the organization is operated every day. Leaders are held accountable for meeting all objectives. These are the critical ingredients in integrating operating systems and risk management in a coordinated manner. This combination of risk management and management systems standards was not in place until 2012. The International Organization of Standardization is currently reviewing the HLS and will report its findings in 2021.

Notes

1. ISO (2015).
2. ISO (2013).
3. ISO (2015).

References

Australian Government, Department of Finance. 2016. "Risk Management Process." https://finance.gov.au/sites/default/files/comcover-information-sheet-undertaking-the-risk-management-process.pdf (accessed April 6, 2019).

Baker, L. 2018. *Practical Enterprise Risk Management.* Lake Mary, FL: Internal Audit Foundation.

Canadian Standards Association. 2010. *Risk Management: Implementation of CAN/ISO 31000.* Toronto: CSA Group.

COSO (Committee of Sponsoring Organizations of the Treadway Commission). 2013. "Guidance on Internal Control." https://coso.org/Pages/ic.aspx (accessed April 6, 2019).

COSO (Committee of Sponsoring Organizations of the Treadway Commission). 2017. *Enterprise Risk Management: Integrating with Strategy and Performance.* Durham, NC: Association of International Certified Public Accountants.

COSO (Committee of Sponsoring Organizations of the Treadway Commission). 2017a. "Enterprise Risk Management: Integrating with Strategy and Performance." *Executive Summary,* https://coso.org/Documents/2017-COSO-ERM-Integrating-with-Strategy-and-Performance-Executive-Summary.pdf (accessed April 6, 2019).

Ethical Trading Initiative. 2018. "The ETI Base Code." https://ethicaltrade.org/sites/default/files/shared_resources/ETI%20Base%20Code%20%28English%29.pdf (accessed April 6, 2019).

Frigo, M.L., and R.J. Anderson. 2014. "What is Strategic Risk Management?" *Strategic Finance,* http://markfrigo.org/What_is_Strategic_Risk_Management_-_Strategic_Finance_-_April_2011.pdf (accessed April 6, 2019).

Hillman, D. 2014. "Managing Overall Project Risk." https://pmi.org/learning/library/overall-project-risk-assessment-models-1386 (accessed April 6, 2019).

Hopkin, P. 2012. *Fundamentals of Risk Management: Understanding, Evaluating and Implementing Effective Risk Management.* London, UK: Kogan Page.

Insurance Institute of Ireland. 2014. "Introduction to Insurance." https://iii.ie/upload/quals-exams/PDI01_Textbook_Sample.pdf (accessed April 6, 2019).

IRM (Institute of Risk Management). 2018. *A Practitioners Guide to ISO 31000:2018.* London: Institute of Risk Management.

ISO (International Organization for Standardization). 2009. *Risk Management—Risk Assessment Techniques, ISO 31010.* Geneva: International Organization for Standardization.

ISO (International Organization for Standardization). 2009a. "Risk Management Vocabulary." *ISO Guide 73*, http://ehss.moe.gov.ir/getattachment/73bc1a52-b3c5-410a-bd2d-cce9edd58652/ISO-iec-guide73 (accessed April 6. 2019).

ISO (International Organization for Standardization). 2013. "Annex SL Concept Document." http://services.accredia.it/UploadDocs/5979_ISO_TMB_JTCG_N0360_N360_JTCG__concept_document_to_support_An.pdf (accessed April 6, 2019).

ISO (International Organization for Standardization). 2014. *Quality Management Systems: Fundamentals and Vocabulary, ISO DIS 9000*. Geneva: International Organization for Standardization.

ISO (International Organization for Standardization) 2015. "Directives—Consolidated ISO Supplement. 2015." *ISO High-Level Structure. Annex SL Appendix 2*, https://fenix.tecnico.ulisboa.pt/downloadFile/1126518382176416/Int5%20-%20Annex_SL_2015.pdf (accessed April 6, 2019).

ISO (International Organization for Standardization). 2015a. *Environmental Management Systems—Requirements with Guidance for Use, ISO 14001*. Geneva: International Organization for Standardization.

ISO (International Organization for Standardization). 2018. *Risk Management—Guidelines, ISO 31000*. Geneva: International Organization for Standardization.

ISO (International Organization for Standardization). 2018a. *Occupational Health and Safety Management System—Requirements with Guidance for Use, ISO 45001*. Geneva: International Organization for Standardization.

Ittner, C., and D. Larcker. 2000. "Non-Financial Performance Measures: What Works and What Doesn't." https://knowledge.wharton.upenn.edu/article/non-financial-performance-measures-what-works-and-what-doesnt/ (accessed April 6, 2019).

Jordan, A. 2013. *Risk Management for Project Driven Organizations*. Plantation, FL: J. Ross Publishing.

Mehr, R.I., and B.A. Hedges. 1963. "Risk Management in the Business Enterprise." https://worldcat.org/title/risk-management-in-the-business-enterprise/oclc/1516965 (accessed April 6, 2019).

Pojasek, R.B. 2017. *Organizational Risk Management and Sustainability: A Practical Step-by-Step Guide*. Boca Raton, FL: CRC Press.

Pojasek, R,B. 2018. "Risk and Risk Management Can Help an Organization Embrace Sustainable Development." *LinkedIn Pulse*, https://linkedin.com/pulse/risk-management-can-help-organization-embrace-bob-pojasek/ (accessed April 6, 2019).

Serrat, O. 2010. "Bridging Organizational Silos." https://digitalcommons.ilr.cornell.edu/intl/120/ (accessed April 6, 2019).

Standards Australia, Standards New Zealand. 2004. *Risk Management Guidelines, HB 436:2004*. Sydney, Australia: Standards of Australia International Ltd.

Standards Australia, Standards New Zealand. 2013. "Risk Management Guidelines—Companion to AS/NZS ISO 31000:2009." https://infostore. saiglobal.com/en-us/Standards/SA-SNZ-HB-436-2013-119721_SAIG_AS_ AS_250882/ (accessed April 6, 2019).

Williams, C.A., and R.H. Heins. 1964. "Risk Management and Insurance." https://worldcat.org/title/risk-management-and-insurance-by-ca-williams-and-rm-heins/oclc/773235271 (accessed April 6, 2019).

About the Author

Robert B. Pojasek, PhD having worked for SAI Global (Sydney), the firm known for its pioneering work for the world's first risk management standard, AS/NZS 4360 in 1995, Bob Pojasek is recognized for his work having transcended the boundaries of traditional verticalized business models to find success working with a wide range of clients globally, cross-continental and regionally. He advocates for using risk management within the *High-Level Structure* (Annex SL) that accommodates the integration of a large number of international standards used to improve the practice of sustainable development for global brand leaders, vertical industry innovators, and technology developers.

Now, once again, Pojasek is operating at the cusp of an emerging transformational period in which organizational leaders are forced to quickly improve their knowledge and leadership scope to navigate the current chaos and contrived disruption that has permanently altered the risk landscape. With it, we see changes to the most fundamental formulas required for business success.

Pojasek has extensive working knowledge of the international standards preferred by corporate investors and Boards for complying with their supply chain protocols, as well as with the only International Standard on Risk Management used by many world companies to comply with their stock exchanges. He was trained in the Australian risk management system (AS/NZS 4360:2004), the first national risk management system in the world, which became the global risk management framework in ISO 31000 in 2009. Among his years consulting for a wide range of clients and experiences, he has conducted risk management, process improvement and management system implementation projects at more than 200 facilities for a range of preferred global supplier organizations.

Pojasek was a founding faculty team member for the *Sustainability Program* at Harvard University's Division of Continuing Education. After 17 years, he is still teaching an online course on organizational risk management and sustainability at the graduate level. He wrote the textbook for the course, *Organizational Risk Management and Sustainability: A Practical Step-by-Step Guide.* Pojasek has served as the thesis director for 26 students and has been honored, at Harvard, with the receipt of the *Petra T. Shattuck Excellence in Teaching Award.*

He is highly regarded for his many years of personal commitment to industry advancements, having served as a Founding Board Member of the Corporate Responsibility Association and International Society of Sustainability Professionals, as well as serving on the Social Responsibility Design Team for the American Society for Quality, the STEM Advisory Board at the Society for Manufacturing Engineers, and Board President of the American Institute for Pollution Prevention.

Pojasek is Senior Strategist at Strategic Impact Partners serving as a co-architect and co-innovator on SIP's ethical trade/sourcing initiative and its broader impacts on growth and valuation. He leads onsite training, strategy development and implementation in risk management for clients utilizing the new SIP ethical trade/sourcing SaaS platform.

You can get more information on risk and risk management on the book's website: http://BringChangeNow.com

Index

OTHER TITLES IN OUR BUSINESS LAW AND CORPORATE RISK MANAGEMENT COLLECTION

John Wood, Econautics Sustainability Institute, Editor

- *Preventing Litigation: An Early Warning System to Get Big Value out of Big Data* by Nelson E. Brestoff and William H. Inmon
- *Understanding Consumer Bankruptcy: A Guide for Businesses, Managers, and Creditors* by Scott B. Kuperberg
- *The History of Economic Thought: A Concise Treatise for Business, Law, and Public Policy, Volume I: From the Ancients Through Keynes* by Robert Ashford and Stefan Padfield
- *Buyer Beware: The Hidden Cost of Labor in an International Merger and Acquisition* by Elvira Medici and Linda J. Spievack
- *The History of Economic Thought: A Concise Treatise for Business, Law, and Public Policy, Volume II: After Keynes, Through the Great Recession and Beyond* by Robert Ashford and Stefan Padfield
- *European Employment Law: A Brief Guide to the Essential Elements* by Claire-Michelle Smyth
- *Corporate Maturity and the "Authentic Company"* by David Jackman
- *Conversations in Cyberspace* by Giulio D'Agostino

Announcing the Business Expert Press Digital Library

Concise e-books business students need for classroom and research

This book can also be purchased in an e-book collection by your library as

- a one-time purchase,
- that is owned forever,
- allows for simultaneous readers,
- has no restrictions on printing, and
- can be downloaded as PDFs from within the library community.

Our digital library collections are a great solution to beat the rising cost of textbooks. E-books can be loaded into their course management systems or onto students' e-book readers.
The **Business Expert Press** digital libraries are very affordable, with no obligation to buy in future years. For more information, please visit **www.businessexpertpress.com/librarians**. To set up a trial in the United States, please email **sales@businessexpertpress.com**.

www.ingramcontent.com/pod-product-compliance
Lightning Source LLC
Chambersburg PA
CBHW061835220326
41599CB00027B/5287